Spiritual Healing

making peace with your past

Michael Sage Hider

WINEPRESS WP PUBLISHING

Packaged by WinePress Publishing, PO Box 428, Enumclaw, WA 98022. The views expressed or implied in this work do not necessarily reflect those of WinePress Publishing. Ultimate design, content, and editorial accuracy of this work are the responsibilities of the author.

The quotation from *Man's Search for Meaning* by Victor Frankl is used by permission of Beacon Press Publishers.

The quotations concerning Dave Thomas are taken from the book *Well Done!* by Dave Thomas with Ron Beyma. Copyright © 1994 by R. David Thomas. Used by permission of Zondervan Publishing House.

The quotations concerning Sam Huddleston are taken from the book, *Five Years To Life* by Sam Huddleston. Copyright © 1991 by Samuel Huddleston. Used by permission of Pneuma Life Publishing.

Scripture excerpts marked NAB are taken from the New American Bible with revised New Testament and Psalms, Copyright © 1991, 1986, 1970 Confraternity of Christian Doctrine, Inc., Washington, DC. Used with permission. All rights reserved. Emphasis added by author.

Verses marked NIV are taken from the Holy Bible, New International Version, Copyright © 1973, 1978, 1984, by the International Bible Society. Used by permission of Zondervan Publishing House. The "NIV" and "New International Version" trademarks are registered in the United States Patent and Trademark Office by International Bible Society. Emphasis added by author.

Verses marked NKJV are taken from the New King James Version, Copyright © 1979, 1980, 1982 by Thomas Nelson, Inc., Publishers. Used by permission. Emphasis added by author.

ISBN 1-57921-202-6
Library of Congress Catalog Card Number: 99-63467

FOR THE GREATER GLORY OF GOD

ACKNOWLEDGMENTS

I thank God, my constant Companion, for all He has given me, for sharing with me the concepts of the Good Life Truths and Healing Steps, and for guiding me in the writing of this book.

I am eternally grateful to my Lebanese father and Italian mother, Sage and Adeline, who gave me not only life, but more for instilling in me an undeceiving spiritual and philosophical self. Few parents have given so much. I felt your spirits talking to me as this book flowed out. Thank you.

I am deeply indebted to my lovely and loving wife, Eileen, and our extraordinary children—Jeffery, Jennifer, Dr. Steven Sage, and Melissa—for all they taught me as we grew up together.

A prodigious thanks to Marvelous Marvin Brown, Bill Newman, and Paul Salvadori, who have greatly enriched my life with their friendship, and for their truehearted criticisms as we collectively read this book. You gentleman will never know how obliged I am to you, nor how much I love you.

To Dr. Cynthia Hunt for her immeasurable assistance in critiquing this book. God sent you as a blessing to me.

But with undying gratitude, I especially thank Jeanne Temple, my literary guide, who breathed life into what could have been a dull book.

CONTENTS

PART ONE

AN OVERVIEW

CHAPTER ONE

PARKED UNDER
THE CHERRY TREE

Imagine yourself seated in the plush leather driver's seat of your recently purchased luxury automobile. The super-powerful motor idles quietly, so smoothly you can't feel it running. The gear-shift selector indicates "Drive." Your foot presses solidly on the brake pedal.

You are stopped on a beautiful country knoll. No one else is in sight. Your favorite song is warbling through the car's wrap-around, stereophonic system.

A brilliant and sparkling sun warms the day. The cloudless sky has never been so blue. The fields are quilted with multicolored wild flowers. Deer, rabbits, and squirrels frolic everywhere.

Pure bliss? Not quite.

Unfortunately, you *chose* to stop under a large cherry tree overflowing with birds. The birds are ravenously devouring the ripe fruit. Nature takes its course. *Plop. Plop. Plop.*

You feel trapped inside. You keep using your windshield washer and wipers in an attempt to see through the windshield to the beautiful world outside. It is of no use—nothing but a big, ugly smear.

Life looks and feels crappy. You are wrought with rage and anger. *Plop. Plop. Plop.*

Shouldn't you move your foot from the brake pedal to the accelerator and use the awesome power available to you to escape this dreadful situation? Shouldn't you zoom down the beautiful road of life delighting in God's incomparable creations? But you don't. You just sit there. *Plop. Plop. Plop.*

Disgusting? Repulsive? Sickening? You bet it is! However, as you will see, there is a reason for using this explicit metaphor. The tale makes an important point.

You say to me, "That seems like an unbelievable story. No one with a new luxury car would park under a cherry tree filled with defecating birds. If she did, she'd leave after the first splatter. She certainly wouldn't just sit there. At least I know I would never be so foolish as to remain at a standstill when I had all that power at my command. I *would* move my foot from the brake pedal, put it on the accelerator and press down hard. Like greased lightning I would streak away from underneath that despicable cherry tree. I would fly carefree down the beautiful road of life. No plop, plop, plop for me!"

Maybe.

Because of past trauma, many people unnecessarily feel trapped by their thoughts. If you are presently disturbed by blustering thoughts of what someone did to you in your past, of that really stupid thing you did, or what Fate did to you, you may be like the driver in our narrative. You have tremendous Power at your command that you may not be using to overcome the agonizing and hurting memories of a past event. Emotionally and unwittingly you may be parked under your own noxious cherry tree. *Plop. Plop. Plop.*

Past trauma can come in many forms: Were you physically or sexually molested as a child? Are you trying to recover from an acrimonious divorce? Do you often think of that incredibly crass thing you did a few years ago? Are you guilty of domestic violence? Do you constantly relive the day when your only child died of some terminal illness? Did you intentionally or negligently kill another person? Are the thoughts of anything that happened in your past tearing you apart? If so, our little story may not be so absurd.

Thoughts of past trauma are analogous to the birds in the cherry tree. Such thoughts make us feel just as trapped and distressed as our driver friend in the above anecdote. I've been there. I've done that. *Plop. Plop. Plop.* But, it doesn't have to be that way.

We intuitively know that we should never let thoughts of any past event tear us asunder. We also intuitively know that we deserve the greatest of all treasures: enduring peace of mind, the perpetual feeling of contentment, forever free from any disturbing thoughts about past events. Unfortunately, we don't know how to deal with our past, nor do we know how to obtain enduring peace of mind.

What frustrates us is knowing it can be done. We are cognizant of people with ghastly pasts, much worse than we experienced, who are now content. They transcended past traumas. Why can't we be like them? Why can't we transcend our past traumas? We wonder how we can get to where they are. How much we would give to be like them!

We can be. Enter God.

We know our God is a God of incredible love. He does not want our preoccupation with thoughts of past events to destroy the peace of our present moment. He wants us to be at peace individually and with Him at all times, including right now. God wants us to always possess enduring peace of mind, His contentment at the center of our being. He has given us the awesome Power to possess enduring peace of mind. His message is unequivocal.

Jesus said:

> Come to Me, all you who are *weary* and *burdened* and I will give you *rest*. (Matthew 11:28 NIV)

Certainly, Jesus is not talking about being *physically* weary and burdened and He will give us rest. A good night's sleep refreshes anyone who is physically weary and burdened. We don't need Jesus to obtain that type of rest. No, Jesus is talking about being *spiritually* and/or *mentally* weary and burdened. And He tells us that our rest, *our enduring peace of mind*, comes from Him.

If you are mentally weary and burdened because of something that happened in your past, you have your foot placed solidly on the brake pedal of your mind. You are not drawing upon the *awesome Power*, which already exists within you, to forever make peace with your past and to drive away from your cherry tree!

The Bible has much to say about the Power that already exists within each of us.

Jesus said:

> And I will ask the Father, and he will give you another Counselor to be with you forever, the Spirit of truth. The world cannot accept him, because it neither sees nor knows him. *But you know him, for he lives with you and will be in you.* (John 14:16–17 NIV)

If we learn to draw upon the Power that already exists within us, our lot will change from torment to peace.

> When you look for me, you will find me. Yes, when you seek me with all your heart, you *will* find me with you, says the LORD, and I *will* change your lot . . . (Jeremiah 29:13-14 NAB)

We learn from Scripture that very same Divine Power that created the universe is within each one of us right now.

> In the beginning was the Word, and the Word was with God, and the Word was God. He was with God in the beginning.
> Through him all things were made; without him nothing was made that has been made. In him was life, and that life was the light of men. The light shines in the darkness, but the darkness has not understood it.

There came a man who was sent from God; his name was John. He came as a witness to testify concerning that light, so that through him all men might believe. He himself was not the light; he came only as a witness to the light. The true light that gives light to *every man* was coming into the world. (John 1:1-9 NIV)

Note well! Scripture does not assert that God gives the light to *every Christian*, or *every believer*! Not at all. The light is given to *every* man (and woman)!

I am of the firmest conviction that God gives every person this light at the moment of his or her conception. A small flame that burns within each of us, murderer to Saint. Is this light burning within us the Holy Spirit? Not yet. But it is the light of God, nevertheless. Scripture says so; and who is so foolish as to disagree with Scripture?

This small flame of God which abides in each of us explains why even the most vile person is capable of performing some acts of charity and love.

If we accept Jesus as our Lord and Savior, it is as if we throw gasoline on this small flame. It *explodes* into the fiery Person of the Holy Spirit so that it fills and consumes us with love for Almighty God and our neighbor. As we know, it is a most wonderful happening!

The point is, the Power you need to once and forever heal you of all disturbing thoughts caused by past traumatic events is within you *right now*. This Power is the solution to all your problems. You have at the very least, the light of God, if not the Person of the Holy Spirit living within you. This Force, vibrantly alive within you, can resolve every problem caused by your past.

This is really exciting!

For reasons that will become obvious later, I call this God Who dwells within each of us our God-I (phonetically: God-eye). Every living person has a God-I dwelling within him or her. It is either the small flame of God or the person of the Holy Spirit.

To avoid making this laborious distinction throughout the remainder of this book, and understanding my audience, I will hereafter use the term God-I as synonymous with the Holy Spirit.

For the moment, just accept the fact that there is a God-I within you Whose phenomenal Power can bring you to perfect peace with your past, no matter how bad it is.

Unfortunately, as we all have woefully experienced, Satan often sends one of his agents to dwell within us, to disturb and tempt us. I call this being our Satan-I. One of Satan-I's greatest desires is that we never make peace with our pasts—that we remain filled with anger, rage, and hate because of what happened in our pasts. Satan-I wants us to think unceasingly about those past events that so much disturb us. First, Satan wants to win our minds, then our souls. Then Satan wins. Much more about Satan-I later.

The Good Life Truths

Jesus said:

> And you shall know the truth, and the truth shall make you free. (John 8:32NKJV)

Obviously, Jesus believes it is important that each of us be *free*. But, spiritually and emotionally speaking, what did Jesus mean by each of us being free? I believe it means that a person is in that wonderful state of mind in which he or she is not controlled nor dominated by any person or thing, including one's past, present, or future. It is that state of mind wherein we each make everlasting peace with our respective pasts, are very content in the present, and have no fear or anxiety about the future. We are free of all emotional restraints. We are not carrying any emotional baggage. We feel good about our lives and ourselves. We have God's peace at the center of our beings. That is true freedom.

And how do we attain that state of wonderful equanimity? By knowing the truth.

Allow me to begin this discussion concerning the Good Life Truths with a brief background statement about myself. I graduated from the University of Cincinnati with a bachelor's degree in metallurgical engineering. After graduation I was commissioned into the United States Air Force as a second lieutenant and was soon promoted to first lieutenant. My first assignment was to Eglin Air Force Base in Fort Walton Beach, Florida. As an engineer, I was placed in charge of Hypervelocity Impact Studies. Those studies involved using a very sophisticated apparatus to shoot small, hard projectiles at different type missile nose cones to determine what effect particles in outer space would have upon colliding with various nose cone materials. The goal was to develop the best nose cone material possible. Those experiments required the use of many engineering formulas and equations.

From Eglin, I was transferred to the Nevada Test Site, near Las Vegas, where I assisted in conducting underground nuclear tests. Again, those tests involved the use of many scientific formulas and equations.

After being honorably discharged from the Air Force, I spent a short time in seminary. For many personal reasons I left the seminary. Then, I obtained my master's degree in Philosophy from the University of Toledo. While at the University of Toledo, I met and very much fell in love with Eileen Jones. We married and moved to California. (Thirty-four years later, we're still very much in love!)

In California I first worked as a crystal growing engineer for Fairchild Semiconductor in Mt. View. I then took employment with Lockheed Missiles and Space Company in Sunnyvale, assisting in the development of new materials for Trident Submarine missile re-entry bodies. Throughout those endeavors I continued to use engineering formulas and principles.

To gain more personal freedom I elected to bid farewell to the pursuit of an engineering career to embark on a career in law. While working full-time at Lockheed, I attended and obtained my Juris Doctor degree from Santa Clara University. Our family then moved to Merced, California where I practiced as a trial attorney for eleven years. I then successfully ran for a seat on the

Merced County Superior Court Bench. After fifteen years, I am the senior Superior Court Judge in Merced County.

Because of my engineering career, I spent much of my early life dealing with incontrovertible truths, expressed as formulas. Some of those truths, which you may recognize, include $F=ma$, $Pv=nRT$, $E=IR$, $e=mc^2$, etc. It is because of these unfailing truths that we are able to put astronauts on the moon, take soil samples from the planet Mars, and surf the World Wide Web. I became fascinated with the reliability of these scientific principles, which I used over and over again in my engineering career. But it occurred to me that these truths only deal with the physical universe.

Because of my enginering, seminary, philosophy, and law background, the thought presented itself that possibly God has ordained that our spiritual world be governed by laws as reliable and verifiable as the laws which govern our physical world. I discovered there are such laws or Truths. I call these Truths the Good Life Truths.

Every scientific truth about the physical world begins with a theoretical formula. It is by verifying over and over again the truth of the theoretical formula that it becomes accepted as an inerrant scientific truth. So it is with the Good Life Truths. At my request, a number of people have tested these Truths against life's experiences. The Good Life Truths prove to be as verifiable and inerrant as scientific truths. They are simple statements of Truth that are incontrovertible. Like scientific formulas, they cannot be disputed by any rational person.

I call these Truths the Good Life Truths because they guide us to the good life of enduring peace of mind and contentment, *regardless* of what happened in one's past. In fact, it is only by living these Good Life Truths that we can be free from the negative aspects of our pasts.

Just as we use scientific formulas to understand and deal with the physical world, so we must learn to use Good Life Truths as formulas to understand and deal with the mental world. Once each of us learns the *Truths* about how to deal with one's past, we can forever enjoy God's peace in the present moment. This is what God wants us to do.

Let me introduce you to four Good Life Truths. You will note that each Good Life Truth is couched in the first person singular. I do this for emphasis. When you say "I", say it with gusto! It means you personally.

Say to yourself:

The most valuable thing I can own is enduring peace of mind, a feeling of total contentment, of God's perpetual peace at the center of my being.

I can never possess enduring peace of mind until I make peace with my past.

A divine and awesome Power lives within me. I must learn how to draw upon this incredible Power to make peace with my past.

I must never let the thoughts of what happened in one of my yesterdays destroy the peace of my today.

As you meet each Good Life Truth, study it just as you study each piece of a jigsaw puzzle. Think of each Good Life Truth as a piece of your good life puzzle. These truths are as real as puzzle pieces you hold in your hand. Become familiar with each shape, color, and feel. Let them speak to you.

However, the Good Life Truths are infinitely more valuable than any puzzle pieces comprised of paper, cardboard, and ink. In fact, they are more valuable than diamonds and rubies. The Good Life Truths are the most valuable tools you will ever own because they will bring you the greatest of all treasures—enduring peace of mind.

Throughout this book, we assemble the Good Life Truths like a puzzle to show us the way to the good life. Just like puzzle pieces, the Good Life Truths interlock with each other to bring us contentment and enduring peace of mind. A beautiful picture results when we correctly assemble and use the Good Life Truths as our new way of living.

The Bible commands us to live our lives by order and indisputable moral principles. In addition to the sixty-six books that comprise the Protestant Bible, Catholics have in their Bible seven additional books. One of these books is the wonderful book of Sirach, that I will quote from time to time. If you are a Protestant, I very much encourage you to borrow a Catholic Bible and read the Book of Sirach. It will delight your heart and help us to tear down the horrible walls that separate Catholics and Protestants.

Be consistent in your thoughts. (Sirach 5:12 NAB)

By living the Good Life Truths, we become ordered and consistent in our thoughts. We have scientific mental Truths to live by, and the Truth will set us free from our pasts. We have a never failing method to overcome adverse thoughts about past events. We courageously face adversity and grow because of it. We live above anger and guilt. We exist at a higher level of consciousness. We learn that no past event can ever hurt us again. We learn to control our thought dwelling; therefore, we learn to control our feelings. Our puzzle comes together. We find beauty and contentment in our world. We are not parked under a cherry tree.

As you will see, The Good Life Truths provide us with a way of thinking that is in accordance with God's will, which leads us to make correct choices. In the sense that it is our choice to use or not use the Good Life Truths, God has left the awesome responsibility of possessing enduring peace of mind up to each one of us. I assure you, by living the Good Life Truths, you will come to a deeper abiding faith in God and His faithfulness to you.

If we just look for, recognize, and *choose* to draw upon the stupendous Force of Almighty God, Who dwells within each of us, by *choosing* to live the Good Life Truths, we launch ourselves on a journey of inner peace and contentment. It is a most wonderful journey.

By living the Good Life Truths, you will come to know and love the God within you. You come to know that your God-I is the mighty

Force that empowers you to perpetually defeat Satan. Knowing that the Force is available to you for the *choosing*, you ultimately come to realize that the only person who can prevent you from being content is yourself. As you shall see, no one else nor any event is ever to *blame* if you are not at peace in the present moment. Regardless of your past, it *doesn't* matter!

When I say this, please understand I am not belittling as something trivial the trauma of domestic violence, an acrimonious divorce, rape, child molestation, the death of a loved one, or killing or seriously injuring another person. These are not trivial matters. They are horrific.

But horrific is not the issue. The issue is, are we going to allow the thoughts of such events to negatively affect us and our relationships year after agonizing year for the rest of our lives? Or, are we going to do as God commands? Are we going to once and for all deal with the *thoughts* of the past trauma so they never again destroy our peace in the present moment? By using the term "deal with," I certainly do not mean sweep the thoughts under the rug. In fact, I wish to emphatically stress this last point. If anywhere in this book you believe I am suggesting that you sweep all thoughts of a past trauma under the rug, you are misreading the text. Please carefully reread the passage.

Back to the issue of dealing with or not dealing with the disturbing thoughts of a past event. That is the all-important question. Being at peace with one's past or at war with one's past is *self-determined*. In either event, we do it to ourselves.

By knowing and living the Good Life Truths, you can dispose of traumatic thoughts and feelings that heretofore crushed your peace of mind. That is quite different from stoically accepting the trauma that entered your life. If you live the Good Life Truths you will go through life free from feelings of guilt, hate, and preoccupation about your past. Instead, you will experience present feelings of self-love, love of others, self-esteem, and self-respect. You will forever live in the present, not in the past.

In the Appendix, I compile all the Good Life Truths taken from the summary at the end of each chapter. By periodically reviewing and perpetually living these Good Life Truths you keep yourself at peace and in tune with God. You remain free from disturbing thoughts about your past. I heartily encourage you to read the Summary of Good Life Truths over and over again. Depending on the completeness of your puzzle, you may want to read them daily. Their continued use guarantees the good life.

Dealing with Your Past

Mental health practitioners are fond of talking about "dealing with" past trauma. We hear well-meaning friends and relatives say, "You've got to get that behind you." Sometimes it is, "You must get on with your life," or "Be a winner not a loser." What does all that mean?

"Dealing with," "getting that behind you," "getting on with your life," and "winning," in the form of a Good Life Truth, means the following:

> I know I have overcome the crippling effects of the memory of a past event when I can think about that event and it no longer has a debilitating emotional impact on me. The once highly disturbing memories of that event become nothing more than memories of an historical event, virtually void of emotion. When I attain that state of mind, I am healed.

This is our goal: That you can think of any negative event from your past life and it no longer produces any bad feelings, rage, anger, hate, or discontentment. When you can think about every negative event of your past life in historical terms only, essentially void of emotion, then you have made peace with your past.

Psychiatrists, psychologists, and counselors may be very important to get you started on the correct path to making peace with your past. But ultimately, you and God-I are going to have to bravely face and deal with the thoughts of these past traumatic events. You will be well armed and prepared to accomplish this Herculean task. Never forget:

I can do everything through him who gives me strength. (Philippians 4:13 NIV)

For our well-being, we must learn to quickly transform the emotionally disturbing memories of any past event into memories of nothing more than an historical event. That includes memories of physical abuse, sexual abuse, the death of a loved one, or one's own stupid acts. That is what our All-powerful God wants us to do. For our own well-being, that is what we are obligated to do.

Soon you will be saying, "That did happen to me, but I am happy to tell you that *thinking* about it no longer tears me apart. I have *made peace* with my past." This state of mind is reached by drawing upon the power of the Holy Spirit Who already dwells within you.

I'm not saying attaining that goal is easy. I'm saying with self-discipline it can be accomplished. The price you pay, which is continually living the Good Life Truths, is well worth the resulting peace of mind you will possess.

Speaking of one's past, there is much to be said about the characteristics of what we erroneously call "the past." Although you may doubt it now, please bear with me and let me present my case, I will prove to you that "the past" does not exist (except in the mind of God where it is really the present). Further, we must come to realize that the thing we each call our individual past is unchangeable, it is feelingless and it cannot possibly hurt us *without* our permission.

I provide a chapter Synopsis at the end of each chapter. For emphasis, it is also couched in the first person singular.

Let us drive away from under the cherry tree.

God's peace be with you.

Synopsis

Say to yourself:

For much too long, I have let memories of what another person did to me, of that really stupid thing I did, or of what Fate did to me ruin my peace of mind in the present moment. That must stop. Somehow I know that I am the only person who can bring this affliction to an end. Somehow I know there is a Power within me that can assist me in my struggle. I must learn to draw upon this Power. I must learn how to be *free* finally and forever from debilitating thoughts about any event from my past life. I must never again mentally park under that despicable cherry tree!

GOOD LIFE TRUTHS
DERIVED FROM CHAPTER ONE

1-1. The most valuable thing I can own is enduring peace of mind, a feeling of total contentment, of God's perpetual peace at the center of my being.

1-2. I can never possess enduring peace of mind until I make peace with my past.

1-3. A divine and awesome Power lives within me. I must learn how to draw upon this incredible Power to make peace with my past.

1-4. I must never let the thoughts of what happened in one of my yesterdays destroy the peace of my today.

1-5. I know I have overcome the crippling effects of the memory of a past event when I can think about that event and it no longer has a debilitating emotional impact on me. The once highly disturbing memories of that event become nothing more than memories of an historical event, virtually void of emotion. When I attain that state of mind, I am healed.

CHAPTER TWO

MARY, PAMELA, AND THE REST OF US

When I was an attorney one of my specialties was family law. As such I handled more than a thousand divorce cases. I marveled at the tremendous difference in how my clients reacted to their respective divorces. For example:

Luminary Mary

Mary is one of the nicest ladies I know. It was a tremendous pleasure having her as a client. Mary and her husband were farm laborers. They worked seasonally. When not doing farm labor, they did odd jobs.

Unfortunately, Mary's husband was an alcoholic. When inebriated, which was often, he became mean and abusive. He was also a compulsive gambler. He lost most of the money he earned at local poker tables.

Mary had been to my office several times to consult about a dissolution of her marriage. She was opposed to divorce, but her marriage was insufferable. At the conclusion of each visit, I provided her with the necessary forms to commence her divorce. We would set her next appointment, which she would cancel and I would then not see her for a long period of time. It almost became a ritual. That is until one day when she returned, papers in hand, and two black eyes.

In Mary's words, "The beatings are getting much worse than they used to be. Before, he wouldn't hit me in front of the children, now he does. I truly believe he hates me. You know, I probably still would not divorce him, except I learned he has an ongoing affair with my best friend. Apparently everyone knew of the affair except me. I guess that's typical. If it wasn't for my faith in God, I don't know what I would do."

We proceeded with the dissolution of Mary's marriage. She was granted custody of her four children, ages fourteen, twelve, ten, and eight. There was no real estate and only a paucity of personal property to divide.

Mary's ex-husband left the area and was seldom heard from after the divorce. That was many years ago. There were no aggressive child support enforcement laws at that time. Mary was left destitute with four children to raise.

Mary spent the next ten years working endlessly to care for her children with no financial or moral support from their father. When she and the older children did farm work, Mary would take the younger children with her to the field at 4:00 A.M. She couldn't afford daycare nor a babysitter.

I occasionally see Mary around Merced. I never pass up the opportunity to speak to her. It is a thrill to do so. What amazes me is her never-ending, positive attitude and her enduring peace of mind. Mary does not complain about her ex-husband or their marriage. Quite the contrary, she only comments how fortunate she is that he gave her four beautiful children who love her so much. Her *thoughts* are about all the good he gave her in the form of these children. Since she carries no bad *thoughts* about her former husband, she has no bad *feelings* toward him. There is no hate in Mary's heart.

I last saw Mary at our local post office. Now in her mid-sixties, she is badly bent and uses a cane. As we walked to her faded old car with tattered seats, we had the following conversation:

"Mary, how are you feeling?"

"Oh, my arthritis is trying to get the better of me, but I'm not going to let it." Her response did not surprise me. That is vintage Mary. In obvious agony, she continued to limp toward her car.

"How are your children?"

Her face took on a radiant glow. "Oh, Judge Hider, they're wonderful! The three oldest children are happily married and have good jobs. I have two beautiful grandchildren. My baby is a college graduate. I'm so proud of them. They treat me so well. God has been so *good* to me!"

Mary gave me a big hug and twisted painfully into the driver's seat of her car. We said good-bye. Waving, with a big smile on her face she drove the belching vehicle away. I waved back with tears of love and admiration in my eyes.

Clearly, Luminary Mary is not parked under a cherry tree. She is zooming down the beautiful road of life, enjoying all God has given her. It is not so with Pamela.

Perturbed Pamela

Eileen and I had a casual social relationship with Pamela and her doctor-husband, Bob. It was obvious they were becoming more discordant as time went on. Finally, Pamela retained me to commence a dissolution action against Bob.

Even though California is a no-fault divorce state, clients often insist on telling their attorneys why they are filing for divorce. Pamela is one of those type people.

What was so interesting is that I was handling Pamela's and Mary's cases at the same time. There, the similarity ended. I never handled two cases that were more diametrically opposed.

During our discussions I asked Pamela if Bob had ever struck her? "Oh no, he would never do that." How about cheating on her? "Not once; he's too religious to commit adultery." Was he stingy with money? "No, I can buy whatever I want."

Sensing I was somewhat perplexed, Pamela retorted, "You just don't understand!" She was correct. "Bob is either in his office or at the hospital most of each day. It's like not having a husband."

Pamela was a nurse before she married Bob. I asked her, "Being a nurse, didn't you realize what it would be like being a doctor's wife?"

"Yes, but . . ."

"And isn't it true that each year you and Bob take several lengthy vacations with the entire family?"

"Yes, but . . ."

"Is Bob a bowler, golfer, gambler?"

"No, but . . ."

"When he's home does he spend time with the family?

"Yes, but . . ."

Since none of the "buts" were valid answers, I could not resist pressing on, "But what?"

"His horizons are so limited! It's just work and family. Before we were married, we did so many things together. Whatever I wanted to do, Bob would do. I thought when we got married there would be a nonstop series of operas, concerts, ballets, and trips abroad. But, that's not at all the way it is. There is so much out there I want to experience. Bob could care less. Now with his growing practice and the time he spends with the children, I feel left out. And he doesn't care. And our sex life is really in the tank.

"When I ask him why he is treating me this way, he doesn't even know what I'm talking about. There is so much more to marriage than what I have. Bob has absolutely no interest in taking care of my needs."

I inquired, "How about counseling?"

"It's out of the question. I'm convinced there is no use continuing in this marriage."

We proceeded with Pamela's divorce.

Bob had made many wise investments. As her share of the community property, Pamela received their resplendent home with its beautiful furnishings, a lot of commercial real estate, her luxury automobile, and a million dollars in cash. Her monthly income far exceeds what most people in our small town of Merced earn in a year. She will never have to work, regardless of her lifestyle.

Bob paid the college expenses for their two daughters. He was always there when they needed him. They would tell you he is an excellent father.

The dissolution of her marriage did not help Pamela. She remains bitter. She will never forgive Bob for, as she says, "What he did to me." That is all Pamela wants to talk about.

Let's compare Luminary Mary and Perturbed Pamela.

Mary had a deplorable marriage. Her husband physically and mentally abused her time and time again. He cheated on her, having an ongoing affair with her best friend. He did it openly and without shame. Finally, he squandered their meager resources and left Mary destitute with four children to raise. Mary's former husband contributed nothing to the raising of his children. Yet, Mary is totally unencumbered by her past. She is carrying no emotional baggage. She is truly enjoying her family and her life.

As for Pamela, Bob never physically abused her, nor did she even fear such an act. Bob did not cheat on Pamela nor treat her badly. Money was never a problem, as Pamela had all the money she could spend. Finally, Bob is extremely generous and an excellent father to their daughters.

Although she may drive her *physical* luxury car eighty miles an hour, Pamela's *mental* luxury car is at a dead stop, her foot solidly on the brake pedal, parked under her cherry tree. *Plop. Plop. Plop.*

Why does Mary, who possesses so little, feel so grateful for what she does have? Why is Mary not bitter about her past? Why does Pamela, who possesses so much, physically speaking, feel so discontented and frustrated, despite all she possesses? Why is Pamela so bitter about her past? Why is Mary happily zooming down the beautiful road of life while Pamela persists on sitting beneath her cherry tree?

Being financially rich like Pamela is not necessarily bad. Having enduring peace of mind like Mary, no matter what has happened to you, is much better.

It is most important that you do not miss the point that is made by comparing Mary and Pamela. They both went through the unpleasant experience of a divorce, yet Mary is at peace with her past while Pamela is filled with anger, hate, and discontent. The point I make is that going through a divorce, *in and of itself*, does not cause you to feel a certain way in the present moment.

By comparing Mary and Pamela we can deduce two important Good Life Truths:

> Past events, in and of themselves, cannot cause me to feel unhappy in the present moment. That is because once an event is over, it can no longer hurt me.

> It is negative thinking about past events that hurts me. This is a difference I must never forget. Past events cannot hurt me. Only my negative thinking about past events can hurt me.

There is a spiritual explanation as to why people who have similar past experiences are so different in their present moment thoughts and feelings. There is a spiritual explanation as to why there are Luminary Marys and Perturbed Pamelas in the world. Once you understand what is happening spiritually, you can be a Mary instead of a Pamela *regardless* of what happened in your past life.

Thought Dwelling and Feelings

I am often invited to speak and/or lecture about the subject matter of this book at Professional Persons Breakfasts, Service Club Lunches, College Classes, etc. After introducing my audience to the concept of Good Life Truths, I request that they join me in a most important experiment. Now, I request that you join me in this same experiment.

We begin by relaxing and dwelling on a series of pleasing thoughts. I ask you to personalize and slowly relish these thoughts as they apply to you. I want you to remember:

- Childhood memories of how you enjoyed romping along a beach or frolicking in a winter-wonderland.
- Your first puppy or kitten.
- How proud you felt when you learned how to ride a bicycle.
- The excitement of your first car.
- Your most wonderful birthday.
- Your most joyful Christmas.
- Blossoms in Springtime.
- When you fell in Love.
- Your engagement.
- How beautiful or handsome you looked on your wedding day.
- That exquisite candlelight dinner you assiduously prepared for your lover.
- Floating on a sunset with your spouse snuggled so close that there is only one of you.
- The first time you cuddled and nuzzled a chubby little baby, receiving a bubbly giggle in return.
- Delighting your palate with every delicious bite of your favorite dessert.
- Your appetite being whetted by the alluring aroma of bread baking in the oven.
- The sweet sensation of walking into a flower shop to buy your mate flowers.
- That magnificent Sunday when your favorite football team won the Superbowl.
- The happiest moment of your life.
- The day you turned your life over to Christ.

I then make a request of the audience that I now make of you: "If thinking these thoughts makes you feel good, please physically (or mentally) clap." I am confident you enthusiastically delivered at least a mental applause.

When the applause ends, I pre-apologize to my audiences, as I now pre-apologize to you. What is about to happen is going to be most unpleasant. But it is absolutely necessary to make a point you must never forget!

Now, we are going to dwell on a series of very displeasing thoughts. I ask you to personalize these thoughts as they apply to you. I want you to remember:

- When you were sexually molested.
- When you were physically abused.
- When you were mentally abused.
- When your spouse cheated on you.
- When you cheated on your spouse.
- The horrible divorce you went through.
- Your alcoholism.
- Your use of illegal, controlled substances.
- That really stupid, stupid thing you did for which you can never forgive yourself.
- How Fate has hurt you by fire, flood, failing-health, or the death of a loved one.
- The most horrible thing that ever happened to you.
- What a jerk you are!

I repeat my appeal to my audiences, and to you: "If these thoughts make you feel good, please clap." Nothing, but silence.

I know how dwelling on these negative thoughts makes you feel. I know you are not clapping.

So, what valuable lesson have we learned from this experiment? Burn into your memory and never forget this next Good Life Truth! This is one of the most important of all the Good Life Truths:

> The type of thought I choose to dwell upon determines how
> I feel at any conscious moment of my life.

If we accept the premise that the type of thought one dwells upon causes one's feelings, then when it comes to making peace with one's past, there are only two types of people:

1. People like Luminary Mary who *are in control of their thought dwelling* and therefore are in control of their feelings.
2. People like Perturbed Pamela *who are not in control of their thought dwelling* and therefore are *not* in control of their feelings.

We can have a life of peace and contentment by ridding ourselves of the emotional baggage we may be toting around with us. All we have to do is to learn to draw upon the incredible *Force* of the very real, omnipotent, loving God who lives inside each of us to control our *thought dwelling*. This gives us control of our *feelings*. Then we come to peace with our pasts.

This leads us to an extremely important Good Life Truth. If the thoughts you dwell upon cause your feelings, and you alone are responsible for controlling your thought dwelling, then it necessarily follows that:

> I alone am responsible for how I feel every conscious moment of my life.

Memorize those fourteen words! They can change your life.

To further drive home the relationship between personal responsibility and possessing enduring peace of mind, we extrapolate the last Good Life Truth to the next higher level. In the form of a Good Life Truth this becomes:

> I am the only person who can prevent me from possessing enduring peace of mind. No other person can take enduring peace of mind away from me. Nobody can, just me.

Habits

Another important Good Life Truth deals with habits. Soon, you will realize and accept a simple truth:

The correct habits of mind give me enduring peace of mind. With the correct habits of mind, life may send me challenges, but it can never destroy my enduring peace of mind.

By *correct habits of mind*, I mean habitually governing our lives by the Good Life Truths. We must do that if we want to fully experience God's contentment at the center of our being. There can be no exceptions. If we choose not to habitually live the Good Life Truths, like Perturbed Pamela, our puzzles will never be complete. Habit is the *blood* of the good life. Without good habits we emotionally die just as certainly as we physically die without blood in our bodies.

But what is habit? *Webster's New Collegiate Dictionary* defines habit as follows:

1. A settled tendency or usual manner of behavior
2. A behavior pattern acquired by frequent repetition or physiological exposure that shows itself in regularity or increased facility of performance
3. An acquired mode of behavior that has become nearly or completely involuntary
4. A way of acting fixed through repetition
5. *Habit implies a doing unconsciously and often compulsively*
6. Suggests a fixed attitude or usual state of mind
7. Synonyms are *addiction* and *custom*

Habitually living the Good Life Truths is what the good life is all about. It is a manner of thinking and behavior, a set pattern. It is doing almost involuntarily what we ought to do. We must do it unconsciously and compulsively. Governing our lives by Good Life Truths must become our fixed attitude and usual state of mind, addictively and customarily. As Cicero so eloquently stated, "*Mighty is the force of habit.*"

And how do we develop such inflexible habits? Men much wiser than I have answered that question over the centuries:

OVIDIUS: "Practices become habits."

HORACE MANN: "Habit is a cable; we weave a thread of it everyday, and at last, we cannot break it."

SHAKESPEARE: "How use doth breed a habit in man."

ARISTOTLE: *"We are what we repeatedly do. Excellence, then is not an act, but a habit."*

The good life is not in our possessions, but in our habits. It is in the habits of our minds.

Start weaving a mighty cable right now one Good Life Truth at a time. Constantly review and practice the Good Life Truths over and over again until living them becomes totally habitual. Until this becomes your indisputable way of life, until the good life is your life, until you never again allow negative thoughts of a past event to destroy your present moment peace of mind.

Synopsis

Say to yourself:

I am weary of experiencing feelings of depression, guilt, anger, hate, unhappiness, and discontentment when I think about my past. I want very much to make final and ever-lasting peace with my past. I see people with more dismal pasts than myself that possess present moment enduring peace of mind. They are an inspiration to me. I know that somehow I can transcend my past and get to where they are. I am coming to understand that I transcend my past by drawing upon the awesome God-Force Who dwells at the center of my being. This is the same Force Who created the universe. This is my loving God Who is concerned about my mental well-being. By *habitually* utilizing this Force, I know that regardless of what happened to me in my past, I can overcome it. I can come to total peace with my past. I can possess enduring peace of mind and unceasing contentment in the present moment.

GOOD LIFE TRUTHS
DERIVED FROM CHAPTER TWO

2-1.   Past events, in and of themselves, cannot cause me to feel unhappy in the present moment. That is because once an event is over it can no longer hurt me.

2-2.   It is negative thinking about past events that hurts me. This is a difference I must never forget. Past events cannot hurt me. Only my negative thinking about past events can hurt me.

2-3.   The type of thought I choose to dwell upon determines how I feel at any conscious moment of my life.

2-4.   I alone am responsible for how I feel every conscious moment of my life.

2-5.   I am the only person who can prevent me from possessing enduring peace of mind. No other person can take enduring peace of mind away from me. Nobody can, just me.

2-6.   The correct habits of mind give me enduring peace of mind. With the correct habits of mind, life may send me challenges, but it can never destroy my enduring peace of mind.

PART TWO

THOUGHT DWELLING AND
THE GOOD LIFE

CHAPTER THREE

TAKING CONTROL OF YOUR THOUGHT DWELLING

In Chapter Two I stressed the importance of the following Good Life Truth:

> I alone am responsible for how I feel every conscious moment of my life.

You say, "I'm no fool, I hate to be haunted by turbulent thoughts of things that happened in my past. I want to be like Luminary Mary and not like Perturbed Pamela. I most definitely don't want to be parked under that awful cherry tree. I forever want to put behind me all disturbing thoughts of my past. Vaguely, I understand that I alone am responsible for how I feel every conscious moment of my life. I am willing to accept that responsibility. What else do I need to do?"

You need to unequivocally accept the proposition that the thoughts you dwell upon cause your feelings.

Concerning thought dwelling and resulting feelings, the New American Bible says:

> A word is the source of every deed;
> a thought, of every act.
> *The root of all conduct is the mind*;
> four branches it shoots forth;
> Good and evil, death and life.
> (Sirach 37:16-17 NAB)

To make peace with one's past, we must comprehend the importance of the following concepts:

1. The type of thought a person *consciously or unconsciously* chooses to dwell upon determines how he feels in the present moment.
2. When a person habitually dwells on positive or pleasing thoughts about events from her past, it results in her experiencing positive feelings. She feels contentment. She has God's peace in her heart. By habitually choosing to dwell on positive thoughts, she produces the good life. Like Luminary Mary, if we only dwell on positive thoughts, we have contentment, *regardless* of what life has done to us.
3. When a person habitually dwells on negative or displeasing thoughts about events from his past, it results in his experiencing negative feelings. He becomes negative. He feels hate, anger, guilt, and discontentment. He does not feel good about himself. He is not content. He does not have enduring peace of mind. He is not nice to be around. He is unhappy. He becomes like Perturbed Pamela, no matter how much he possesses in the present moment. In the extreme case, he becomes like Adolf Hitler.
4. Therefore, it cannot be overstated how important it is for a person to learn how to take control of his *thought dwelling* so that he dwells only on positive thoughts about his past,

and immediately and viciously kills negative thoughts about his past. (Please bear with me, the methodology of *how* we control our thought dwelling is the subject of the next chapter.)

Allow me an introductory note to the concept of thought dwelling. There is a profound difference between a thought that spontaneously comes into one's mind, upon which one does not dwell, and a thought that comes into one's mind, upon which one chooses to dwell. Thoughts not dwelt upon are of little consequence. Thoughts dwelt upon are of great consequence and are crucial in determining whether one ever makes peace with one's past, whether one has the good life, the bad life, or somewhere in between.

Let me provide an example of that distinction. There is absolutely nothing wrong for a man to see a woman and to momentarily admire her beauty. To dwell on thoughts of mentally disrobing her and taking her to bed is quite another thing. That is the distinction Jesus was alluding to when He discussed a man committing adultery in his heart with a woman. Jesus said:

> You have heard that it was said, 'Do not commit adultery.' But I tell you that anyone who looks at a woman *lustfully* has already committed adultery with her in his heart. (Matt. 5:27-28 NIV).

That brings us to our next Good Life Truth:

> There is nothing which affects my well-being more than controlling the type of thought upon which I dwell.

It is most tragic that we often go through the process of dwelling on negative, self-defeating thoughts without any realization of what we are doing!

The ability to control the type of thought upon which we dwell is one of the greatest strengths God has given us! It is a stupendous asset in our battle against Satan. Yet, despite the fact that the

Power to control our thought dwelling is within each of us at all times, it is seldom recognized or consciously used.

Generally, the defendants I deal with in the criminal justice system seem to have no clue that their thoughts cause their actions and feelings. Nor do they seem to understand that they alone choose what thoughts they dwell upon and for how long.

Since dwelling only on positive thoughts and rejecting negative thoughts is imperative for coming to peace with one's past, the importance of controlling thought dwelling cannot be overstated.

Thought Origination and Thought Selection

As an essential component of controlling thought dwelling, we must first understand the essence of thought origination and thought selection.

When I give this lecture on thought origination and thought selection, I commence by discussing experiences common to everyone in the room. I ask if there is anyone who ever experienced positive, self-fulfilling thoughts. Of course, all in attendance experienced such thoughts. I then inquire if anyone ever experienced negative, self-defeating thoughts. Again, all in attendance experienced such thoughts.

I continue my interrogation by delving deeper into the concept of dwelling on positive and negative thoughts. Do the thoughts we dwell on affect our personality, our very being? Was Adolf Hitler the person he was because of the thoughts upon which he chose to dwell? Was Mother Teresa the person she was because of the thoughts upon which she chose to dwell? By changing the thoughts upon which he dwelt, could Adolf Hitler have been as holy as Mother Teresa? By changing the thoughts upon which she dwelt, could Mother Teresa have been as vile as Adolf Hitler?

Is there something or someone within each of us that is the source of our good thoughts, which when dwelled upon causes us to feel good? Is there something or someone within each of us that is the source of our evil thoughts, which when dwelled upon causes us to feel badly? I then propose to the audience that the answer to each of those questions is an unqualified and resounding "Yes". I dogmatize that we are who we are because of the *type* of thoughts upon which we habitually choose to dwell.

I then pose the provocative question, "From where do our positive and negative thoughts come?"

Although the room is often filled with professional people, there is seldom a lucid response.

The Anatomy of Our Incorporeal Being

Imagine a friendly alien in a spaceship a million miles from earth contacted you. She wanted to learn as much as possible about human beings before she landed on Earth. You agreed, to the best of your ability, to answer all her questions.

First, she wanted to know what you, a typical human being, looked like. You probably would describe a head with hair, two eyes, a nose, two ears, a mouth, neck, torso, two arms with a hand at each end, two legs with a foot at each end, etc.

Then she requested that you describe your incorporeal being.

What would you answer? A spirit, soul, mind, psyche? It is clearly a problem to describe an incorporeal being, because we have never seen one!

I know that battles go on inside my corporeal body, because I am a prostate cancer survivor. Because of the fight between my good and bad cells, my body weight dropped to 135 pounds. Biopsies revealed that my prostate was filled with cancer. My friend, Dr. Dennis Cesar, performed a radical prostatectomy. Unfortunately for me, residual cancer remained in my body. Because of the outstanding intervention of Dr. Tom Stamey, the radiology health providers at Stanford University Hospital, and God's will, I have been cancer free for over eight years.

However, I know there is an infinitely more grave battle going on right this second and every second of my life inside my incorporeal being. That battle concerns who will get my immortal soul. But, who are the combatants? Certainly not cells.

I know that I have free will, but who is the I that exercises that freewill?

I know that I have a conscience, but which I tells me what is right and what is wrong?

I hesitate to coin new words or phrases, but it is necessary to do so if we are to grasp what transpires in our incorporeal beings. I propose there are many I's within each of us, which explains the use of the following terms.

God-I

One of our I's is a positive I very much interested in maintaining our enduring peace of mind. As set forth in Chapter One, the light of God comes to *every man and woman*, not just to Christians (John 1:9). This light is a positive influence in *everyone's* life. Since the Bible does not indicate otherwise, it is my belief that we each receive this light at the moment of our respective conceptions. Nothing in the Bible contradicts this belief.

I believe that the angel's communique' to Zachariah concerning his son, John the Baptist, corroborates this conviction, with the exception that the light already had become the Holy Spirit:

> He will *also* be filled with the Holy Spirit, *even* from his Mother's womb. (Luke 1:15 NKJV)

Of course, once we accept Jesus as our Lord and Savior, this small flame bursts into the awesome Person of the Holy Spirit and dwells within each of us.

And who is not familiar with those famous passages in 1st and 2nd Corinthians wherein Paul tells us that our bodies are the temples of the living God?

And what did Jesus say the Holy Spirit will do for us?

> But the Helper, the Holy Spirit, whom the Father will send in My name, He will teach you all things, and bring to your remembrance all things that I said to you. *Peace* I leave with you, *My peace* I give to you; not as the world gives do I give it to you. *Let not your heart be troubled, neither let it be afraid.* (John 14:26–28 NKJV)

There can be no question that we are the temples of the Holy Spirit, filled with the Holy Spirit. And we have a supreme Helper. The supreme Power of the universe has been within each of us from the moment of conception, is within each of us now, and will be within each of us through our last breath. Whether you like it or not, you are inseparable from God and He has been a part of your very being since the moment of your conception!

The God-I within each of us is part of the same Power that spoke into being the entire universe. He is the same Force that totally destroyed within two to three weeks Egypt, the world's greatest empire to that time. This God-I is the same Source that ordered the Red Sea to stop, and it humbly obeyed. He is the Healer of all our physical and mental wounds. He is the God who is infinitely greater than any need we will ever have. This Force is the fountainhead of our strength and peace. He is the God of Power and the God of Might. And, yes, this is the very same Omnipotent Being Who comes to us like a beggar and pleads with us to love Him, to trust Him, to place our cares on Him. He is the Awesome God Who lives within you and me! Rejoice!

God has demonstrated His enormous love for each of us by actually giving part of Himself to us. We don't see air, yet we know it is always around and within us. We don't see God, yet we know

He is always around and within us. We each experience the manifestation of air. We each experience the manifestation of God. With air, we physically live. Without air, we physically die. With God as our *chosen* companion, we mentally live. Without God as our *chosen* companion, we mentally die.

Your God-I fills your mind with positive thoughts about yourself, other people, physical events, and situations. Your God-I offers to your mind an endless stream of positive thoughts of jobs well done, self-love, self-esteem, self-worth, self-reliance, self-confidence, love of others, lively birthday parties, joyful weddings, happy Thanksgivings, and merry Christmases with family and friends. Your God-I wants you to feel good, makes you feel good, challenges you to grow, and prompts you toward the good life. We all enjoy the experience of God-I positive thoughts.

Dwelling on your God-I positive thoughts produces good feelings about yourself and your life, *regardless* of your past! God, through God-I wants you to be filled with peace, contentment, love, and a zest for living. It is a Divine experience.

God-I is the part of our human nature that makes us noble, right-minded, and magnanimous. God-I is the part of our human nature that causes us to perform acts of faith, hope, charity, chivalry, honorable deeds, to be altruistic, and to lay down one's life for one's neighbor.

New Agers are preoccupied with discovering the positive force which exists within the world and within each of us. They seek the mighty Power we draw upon to make us invincible against the dark side. They believe when we discover this force, it empowers us to overcome the evil one.

In one way, the New Agers are correct. There is such a Force. He has always existed. He will always exist. He is the Force Who moves the universe. This Force is the Holy Spirit, the Paraclete, the Advocate, God within us. It is God Almighty Himself. This Force is God-I. He makes us invincible against the dark side.

When we draw upon this Force, we are unconquerable. We are empowered to easily overcome the vicious attacks of the evil one, even when the evil one is at his strongest. We become infinitely mightier than the evil one. As St. Paul stated:

> I can do *everything* through him who gives me strength. (Philippians 4:13 NIV)

The only time we can ever be at peace is when we are in union with God through God-I. Obviously, our goal should be to always stay in union with God. We do this by restricting our thought dwelling to God-I thoughts only. That is what the content people of the world know and do. I call this God-I thinking.

Satan-I

Especially in today's world we see people leading exceptionally evil lives. The news media inundates us with stories of domestic violence, murder, cannibalism, rape, child abuse, pornography addiction, hate crimes, epidemic adultery, drug addiction, and alcoholism. It tells us of a seven year old boy and eight year old boy murdering an eleven year old girl for her bicycle, an eleven year old boy and thirteen year old boy brutally gunning down a teacher and their own classmates in the school playground, the horror at Columbine High School where two heavily armed students killed twelve schoolmates and a teacher before killing themselves, etc. What is the source of this evil within us? Many would say it is just human nature. They are correct. It is our human nature. There is no other plausible explanation. That leads us to our second I, whom you also met in Chapter One.

Our second I is a negative I, hell bent on destroying our enduring peace of mind and our life everlasting. I call this I our Satan-I.

Just as surely as God lives within each of us, Jesus tells us that Satan's agents also come to live within each of us. Jesus said:

> For from within, out of the heart of men, proceed *evil thoughts*, adulteries, fornications, murders, thefts, covetousness,

wickedness, deceit, lewdness, an evil eye, blasphemy, pride, foolishness. All these evil things come from within and defile a man. (Mark 7:2123 NKJV)

Why do you not understand My speech? Because you are not able to listen to My word. You are of your father the devil, and the desires of your father you want to do. He was a murderer from the beginning and does not stand in the truth, because there is no truth in him. When he speaks a lie, he speaks from his own resources, for he is a liar and the father of it. (John 8:4344 NKJV)

And what is it that Satan wants to do with us?

Be sober, be vigilant; because your adversary the devil walks about like a roaring lion, seeking whom he may devour. Resist him, steadfast in the faith, knowing that the same sufferings are experienced by your brotherhood in the world. (1 Peter 5:89 NKJV)

Your Satan-I fills your mind with a continuum of negative thoughts about yourself, other people, physical events, and situations. Your Satan-I offers to your mind a never ending stream of thoughts regarding guilt, self-doubt, self-condemnation, self-contempt, self-destruction, low self-esteem, self-hate, ruined anniversaries, forgotten birthdays, lonely holidays, hate of others, incest, rape, and murder. Satan-I negative thoughts are the *weeds* of one's mind.

Dwelling upon your Satan-I negative thoughts makes you feel angry, fearful, guilty, bad about yourself and your life. Dwelling upon Satan-I negative thoughts leads to the use of drugs, the excessive consumption of alcohol, and murder. Satan-I loves it when you dwell upon these self-defeating negative thoughts. Satan-I wants you to feel badly and prompts you toward the negative life of guilt feelings, hate, substance addiction, domestic violence, and pornography. In the worst scenario, dwelling on

Satan-I negative thoughts can destroy you as surely as arsenic can destroy you.

The more Satan-I can ensnare you to dwell upon negative, self-defeating thoughts, the more Satan-I has you in his grip. That causes you to be distracted from all the good things you possess and who you really are, a loved child of God.

I call that Satan-I thinking. My dear friends Bill Newman and Paul Salvadori call it "stinking-thinking".

Thought dwelling is mutually exclusive. You cannot dwell on a God-I positive thought and a Satan-I negative thought at the same time. Obviously, when you make the *choice* to dwell on a Satan-I negative thought, to do stinking-thinking, you also make the *choice* not to dwell on a healthy God-I positive thought for that time of thought dwelling. The result is, instead of feeling positive, you feel negative. Satan-I loves it.

It is Satan-I that is wrong with all of us. Satan-I is the power of darkness within each of us. It is Satan-I within each of us that explains sin and evil in the world. It explains 4000 years of war between Arabs and Jews, between brothers in the same country, between fathers and sons, mothers and daughters, and even between Christians! Satan-I is our most vile and despicable enemy!

My good, loving, positive thoughts come from my God-I. My evil, hateful, negative thoughts come from my Satan-I. There is no other plausible explanation. Besides, as we have seen, Scripture says that's the way it is. Which leads us to the following Good Life Truths:

> Whether I like it or not, God and Satan have been part of my being since the moment of my conception.

> My God-I sends a continuous flow of positive, self-enriching thoughts into my mind. My Satan-I sends a continuous flow of negative, self-defeating thoughts into my mind.

As an aside, George Lucas wasn't quite correct when he developed his marvelous Star Wars Series. He talked about the Force and the dark side of the Force. Indeed, there are two sides to human nature, an enlightened side (God-I) and a dark side (Satan-I). But, they are two unique and separate forces in constant battle with each other for our very souls, not two sides of the same Force.

Choosing-I

A third I, whom I call Choosing-I, has the magnificent power to *choose* whether to accept or reject each God-I or Satan-I thought that enters one's mind and to determine how long to dwell on any thought that is accepted. This is your and my free will. It is not controlled by anything or anybody except the integral you. Not even God Almighty will exercise His power to force Himself upon us and make our respective Choosing-I's dwell only on God-I thoughts and reject all Satan-I thoughts. Of course, for our well-being, that is exactly what we should do every conscious moment of our lives.

Because we have free will, the phenomenal power of God-I cannot help us one iota if we refuse to accept His presence and assistance. When we *choose* Satan-I thinking and reject God-I thinking, the magnanimous Creator of the universe must stand by helplessly and tearfully and watch Satan have his way with us, all to our own destruction.

It is analogous to sitting in our luxury automobile under our infamous cherry tree experiencing bird droppings falling all over us and refusing to draw upon the awesome Power God has given us to escape the situation. It would seem there is no limit to human ignorance. *Plop. Plop. Plop.*

Conscience-I

Many modern day philosophers would have us believe there are no absolute rights or wrongs, that everything is relative. There is a very good reason for the wide-spread popularity of this relativistic philosophy. If we are each god (with a very, very small *g*), then we can each decide for ourselves what is right and what is wrong. Then pornography, fornication, adultery, dope addiction, drunkenness, and making crack babies are all acceptable lifestyles. Also, there is no God to Whom we are all accountable. We can do as we damn please. We are truly free (until Judgment Day!).

This is another one of Satan's sinister devices. The people who fall into Satan's trap of moral relativism are fools. They are destined for destruction in this life and the next life. The philosophy that there are *no absolute* rights or wrongs is *absolutely* ludicrous. We have witnessed the results of abandoning God's laws. It is not a pretty sight.

Let me give you a few absolute wrongs:

- The unlawful taking of another person's life.
- Spousal abuse.
- Rape.
- Exterminating seven million German Jews and forty million Russians, as was done during the first half of the 1900's.
- All genocide.
- To torture to death a one-year-old child just for the pleasure of watching her die.
- The heinous practice of partial birth (ninety-seven per cent born) abortion.
- To sodomize two year old boys just because it brings the perpetrator sexual satisfaction.
- To steal.
- To commit adultery.
- To bear false witness against your neighbor.
- To covet your neighbor's wife.
- To covet your neighbor's goods.

The list is endless.

How does every rational human being know those things are absolutely wrong? They know they are wrong by the reading of

Scripture which imparts knowledge to Conscience-I. As Abraham Lincoln stated:

Without the Bible, we cannot know right from wrong.

God has endowed each of us with a Conscience-I to assist us in our battle against Satan-I. If it were not for our Conscience-I we would not be able to discern whether many of our thoughts were God-I or Satan-I thoughts. Although God was speaking to the House of Israel, His words apply to all of us when He said:

. . . I will put my laws in their minds and write them on their hearts. (Heb. 8:10 NIV).

That is Conscience-I. Because of Conscience-I we know whether any given thought is a God-I or Satan-I thought, and if dwelt upon would lead to our betterment or our detriment.

Once that discernment is made, we must dwell only on God-I positive thoughts and immediately reject all Satan-I negative thoughts, all to our betterment. Of course we are absolutely free to do the opposite. If we do, there are natural flowing consequences, all to our detriment.

Integrated-I

At the very moment of conception, every human being is endowed with the light of God, the darkness of Satan, and the embryos of Choosing-I and Conscience-I. That includes you and me.

We all begin with a perfectly clean slate. We are neither predetermined to favoring God-I thoughts over Satan-I thoughts, nor vice-a-versa. In other words, none of us is predestined to be saint or sinner. That is what free will is all about.

There is no question that the incident of birth has a great effect on how we develop. Very generally speaking, it is mentally and spiritually healthy to be born into a middle-class American home with loving religious parents. Very generally speaking, it is less mentally and spiritually healthy to be born to rich, atheist parents who do not acknowledge absolute right and wrong and live in splendor where there is much confusion about values. It is usually less healthy to be born into a one parent home where that parent is totally consumed with trying to provide the bare essentials for the family. And it is usually less healthy to be born into dire poverty in a place such as Haiti.

But the incident of birth is just one factor in determining who we ultimately become. There are many murderers that come from middle-class, religious American homes. There are many saints in Haiti.

In any event, as we grow, we begin to mature. We slowly grow into the age of reason. That is the age when our Conscience-I gives us the first glimmerings of what is right and what is wrong. We understand that we have choices. We understand that we can *choose* to obey or disobey legitimate authority, *including* God.

We select a peer group, which has a profound effect upon our spiritual growth or retardation. We become like the people with whom we *choose* to associate. That is precisely why it is so important to painstakingly *choose* our associates throughout our lives. But, again, this is just another of the many factors that determine who we become.

At some point in our maturing, regardless of our circumstance of birth or the environment in which we develop, we become cognizant of consequential matters. We become aware of our free will—that we must make choices which profoundly affect us. More importantly, we become aware of God, His attributes and powers. As Scripture tells us:

> The wrath of God is indeed being revealed from heaven against every impiety and wickedness of those who suppress the truth by their wickedness. *For what can be known about God is evident to them, because God made it evident to them.*

Ever since the creation of the world, his invisible attributes of eternal power and divinity have been able to be understood and perceived in what he has made. *As a result, they have no excuse; for although they knew God they did not accord him glory as God or give him thanks.* (Romans 1:18-21 NAB)

With those understandings, we approach full integration. It is a long process.

Finally, as we reach maturity, we become totally integrated. Integrated-I is who each of us is in our entirety. It is more than the combination of our respective God-I, Satan-I, Choosing-I, and Conscience-I. In addition, we are each the memory of our past, our present moment perception of ourselves, our habits of mind, and our expectations and anxieties about our future. We are each the sum of all our physical, mental, and spiritual parts.

More importantly, if we are healthily integrated, we realize and accept our free will. We come to know that through our Choosing-I, we can *choose* to dwell upon or reject every thought that enters our mind, whether it be a God-I positive or Satan-I negative thought. As we mature, we accept full responsibility for our thought dwelling and resulting feelings. We come to the point that we can stop subjectively blaming other people, our past stupid mistakes, or Fate for how we feel in the present moment.

Mother Teresa (obviously my hero) and Adolf Hitler both began with clean slates.

Mother Teresa freely *chose* to habitually do God-I thinking about helping the sick and needy of the world, and rejected Satan-I negative stinking-thinking leading to the salvation of an untold number of souls.

Adolf Hitler was responsible for freely *choosing* to habitually do Satan-I negative stinking-thinking of a superior race and rejecting God-I positive thinking, leading to the useless death of millions of helpless, innocent people. This was such a horrible waste of human life, all because of one man *habitually* dwelling on his Satan-I negative thoughts.

By *choosing* to *habitually* dwell on God-I positive thoughts, of faith, hope, charity, and equal dignity for every human being on the face of the earth, each of us has the ability to become as saintly as Mother Teresa. By choosing to *habitually* dwell on Satan-I negative thoughts of lust, fornication, adultery, rape, hate, anger, and murder, each of us has the ability to become as demonic as Adolf Hitler. *Choosing* the thoughts we dwell upon makes us a Mother Teresa or an Adolf Hitler!

The more your Choosing-I *habitually chooses* to dwell only on God-I positive thoughts, and refuses to dwell on Satan-I negative thoughts, the more you weaken your Satan-I's quantitative and qualitative power over your mind. That is, when your Choosing-I *habitually* rejects Satan-I negative thoughts, the total number, frequency, and intensity of those thoughts will diminish. Slowly, but surely, Satan-I will loose his grip, control, and influence over your mind.

I believe Mother Teresa's Choosing-I and God-I virtually became one, essentially excluding every Satan-I thought at the moment of its inception. That must be our goal.

Of course, everything I said applies with equal but opposite force if we *habitually choose* to dwell only upon Satan-I negative thoughts. One's Choosing-I unites with Satan-I and the mind of that poor soul is filled with nothing but Satan-I negative thoughts.

I believe Adolf Hitler's Choosing-I and Satan-I virtually became one, essentially excluding every God-I thought at the moment of its inception. We must avoid that at all cost.

For many years now, I have been practicing controlling my thought dwelling, as more fully set forth in the next chapter. Although Satan-I never gives up, I assure you that my Choosing-I quickly swats away any Satan-I self-defeating negative thought that enters my mind, using the methodology you will soon be given. I feel my Choosing-I and God-I growing closer together. I feel greater recognition of the Holy Spirit within me. Everyday I grow closer to

God through my God-I. Everyday I rise to a higher level of consciousness. And, I have made everlasting *peace* with my past. My past is historical only, not emotional. In the real sense of the word, I am free.

Satan-I Talk

As another aside, but an important related matter, let me make a bold assertion. We do not spend enough time talking about Satan-I and acknowledging his superhuman powers! And that is very pleasing to Satan!

I see the undeniable presence of Satan, through his Satan-I underlings, in the murderers, rapists, dope users, dope peddlers, and alcoholics with whom I deal. I see him to a lesser degree in my friends. And, although I continue to grow spiritually, I am aware of and still feel his presence in me.

Satan's presence in the world is proven, beyond any reasonable doubt by the break down of the family unit, rampant child abuse, an unprecedented number of teenage pregnancies and unwed mothers, by tens of millions of brutal abortions, sex and violence permeating the media, gangs ruling the streets, unparalelled domestic violence, drive-by shootings, good people prisoners in their own homes behind bars and alarm systems, and unending wars. He knows our individual weaknesses and he stikes at our individual weaknesses.

Satan must be thrilled that the world population is generally ignoring him while he plies his evil. We do not ignore a world pestilence that only kills the body. Yet, we ignore this spiritual plague which destroys human life and sends legions of souls to hell for all eternity, depriving these wretched souls of their celestial home with God. That is sad.

Satan is alive and well. It is extremely important that religious people more vehemently acknowledge his presence and his power. Indeed, we need to spend much more time talking about Satan and his phenomenal powers! That is what I call Satan-I talk. Then, with God's help, he can be defeated in the never-ending battle blustering within each of us. And we defeat him *one person* at a time by defeating the Satan-I in each of us, *one thought* at a time. It is our solemn duty to help each other to do that. That is what God commands. That is how we come to love one's self and one's neighbor. That is how we come to make the world a better place in which to live. That is the legacy we should be leaving to our children.

Obviously, I am very passionate about Satan-I talk and assisting each other to vanquish Satan-I.

But, we must move on.

Throughout this chapter I imply a truth that must be recognized as one of the most important of all the Good Life Truths. That truth is the *centerpiece* of the good-life puzzle. The puzzle pieces that deal with thoughts of the past, present, and future interlock with this centerpiece. That truth is:

> I alone choose how long I dwell upon any thought which enters my mind.

Read this Good Life Truth over a few times. It cannot be over-emphasized. Memorize those fourteen words. They will change your life.

Since we know our thought dwelling produces our feelings, it is obvious that the longer we dwell on negative thoughts, the worse we feel about ourselves, someone else, and life in general. That type of thought dwelling will make life truly miserable.

I offer a supporting anecdote.

Grouchy Jim

Jim is a close friend of mine. He is a retired Air Force officer. He and his former wife, Linda, went through a terrible divorce. Linda receives one-half of Jim's military retirement benefits since those benefits are community property in California. Jim understands that concept and has no problem with it. In his words, "I'm glad I was out flying for twenty years instead of being home raising five kids. Linda did a good job raising our kids."

After their divorce, Jim took on full time employment as a stockbroker. He earns a good income. With his investments, work income, and one-half of his retirement benefits he has no financial worries. He wants for nothing. (Except enduring peace of mind.)

The children have left home. Linda is in excellent health. Although she could work full-time, she elects to work only part-time. Since her income is much less than Jim's, she took him to court seeking spousal support. (Since both of them are friends, I disqualified myself from all their legal proceedings.) The judge ordered Jim to pay Linda spousal support of $400 per month. Based on his total income, that is an insignificant amount and not a financial burden to him.

Unfortunately, Jim is beside himself with rage because of these spousal support payments. He believes Linda should be forced to work full-time, relieving him of any spousal support obligation. It is all he thinks about. It has completely consumed him. He has been back to court three times, facing three different judges, unsuccessfully trying to get his spousal support obligation terminated.

Jim traps me whenever he can. His monologue is always the same. "I don't understand why some judges are so stupid! There is absolutely no reason why Linda can't work full-time! Am I going to pay spousal support until I die? If I could find a guy dumb enough, I'd pay him $25,000 to marry her just so my spousal support obligation would end!"

To no avail, I have tried everything in my power to dissuade Jim from Satan-I stinking-thinking about that insignificant obligation and to dwell upon God-I thoughts of his children and all he does possess. Unfortunately, his Satan-I has a death grip on his mind. Naturally, his hate continues to escalate for Linda, attorneys, and the court system in general. It is a most sad state of affairs. We know where he is parked. *Plop. Plop. Plop.*

Think About Your Thought Dwelling

If you were sexually or physically abused as a child, if you have a medical ailment, if you made bad business decisions, if you went through a horrible divorce, if you committed social faux pas in your past, if you negligently killed another human being, is this what you mostly think about? Do you feel low self-love, low self-esteem, low self-worth, or little self-reliance because of what you did, what another person did, or what Fate did to you? Do you unwittingly quest for other people's pity or are you indulging in your own self-pity? If so, you are *choosing* to dwell upon negative thoughts your Satan-I feeds into you mind. Learn to *habitually* dwell upon positive thoughts God-I feeds into your mind. Viciously kill negative thoughts Satan-I feeds into your mind. Then loving God will give you enduring peace of mind.

That brings us to our final Good Life Truth for this chapter. Although last, it certainly is not the least of the Good Life Truths. In fact, it is one of the most important Truths:

> The key to making peace with my past is to control the type of thoughts upon which I dwell.

Synopsis

Say to yourself:

I realize I have no control over what thoughts spontaneously enter my mind. I also realize I have complete control over how long I dwell upon any thought that enters my mind. I know if I *habitually* choose to dwell upon positive thoughts, it will cause me to feel and act positively. I know if I *habitually* choose to dwell upon negative thoughts, it will cause me to feel and act negatively. Therefore, I confirm the important Truth that by controlling my thought dwelling, *I alone am responsible for how I feel every conscious moment of my life!* Understanding the importance of controlling my thought dwelling leads me a step closer to coming to peace with my past.

GOOD LIFE TRUTHS
DERIVED FROM CHAPTER THREE

3-1.   Whether I like it or not, God and Satan have been part of my being since the moment of my conception.

3-2.   My God-I sends a continuous flow of positive, self-enriching thoughts into my mind. My Satan-I sends a continual flow of negative, self-defeating thoughts into my mind.

3-3.   I alone choose how long I dwell upon any thought which enters my mind.

3-4.   There is nothing which affects my well-being more than controlling the type of thought upon which I dwell.

3-5.   The key to making peace with my past is to control the type of thoughts upon which I dwell.

CHAPTER FOUR

Stop, Obliterate, Alter, Praise (SOAP)

By now you realize there is an unceasing war waging within you between your God-I and your Satan-I. This war has to do with what type of thoughts upon which you are going to dwell. Your God-I desires that you only dwell upon positive thoughts about your past, present, and future. Your Satan-I desires that you only dwell upon negative thoughts about your past, present, and future.

I do not know the rules of this war. I do know, *a priori*, that positive and negative thoughts enter every person's mind, from saint to murderer.

When you *choose* to only dwell upon God-I positive thoughts, you choose the Spirit and the fruits of the Spirit as opposed to the flesh and the fruits of the flesh.

> I say, then: Live by the Spirit (God-I) and you will certainly not gratify the desire of the flesh (Satan-I). For the flesh has desires against the Spirit, and the Spirit against the flesh; these are opposed to each other, so that you may not do what you

want. But if you are guided by the Spirit (God-I), you are not under the law. Now the works of the flesh (Satan-I thought dwelling) are obvious: immorality, impurity, licentiousness, idolatry, sorcery, hatreds, rivalry, jealousy, outbursts of fury, acts of selfishness, dissensions, factions, occasions of envy, drinking bouts, orgies, and the like. I warn you, as I warned before, that those who do such things will not inherit the kingdom of God. In contrast, the fruit of the Spirit (God-I thought dwelling) is love, joy, peace, patience, kindness, generosity, faithfulness, gentleness, self-control. Against such there is no law. Now those who belong to Christ (Jesus) have crucified their flesh (killing all Satan-I thoughts) with its passions and desires. If we live in the Spirit, let us also follow the Spirit (do only God-I thinking). Let us not be conceited, provoking one another, envious of one another. (Gal. 5:16–24 NAB)

You say, "Certainly I desire to live by the Spirit and enjoy the fruits of the Spirit. Further, I want to reject the flesh and not be burdened by the fruits of the flesh. But, how is this accomplished?"

We know that the type of thoughts we dwell upon cause our feelings. If we have no check on our thought dwelling, we have no check on our feelings. We are like an open city with no defense against Satan-I and all the havoc he can wreak upon us. This is especially true when it comes to dwelling on Satan-I negative thoughts about our pasts. In the final analysis making peace with your past is a matter of self-discipline. If you have the self-discipline to perpetually take control of your thought dwelling, then Satan-I is powerless against you. On the other hand, if you do not draw upon the Power that already exists within you to muster this self-discipline, you are powerless against Satan-I.

Are you like a strongly fortified city, or like a city whose walls are broken down? The Bible says:

> Like a city whose walls are broken down is a man who lacks self-control. (Prov. 25:28 NIV).

This leads us to three Good Life Truths:

I have absolutely no control over past events. They are dead and gone forever. However, I have absolute control over how long I dwell upon negative thoughts about past events and the negative feelings that flow therefrom.

Without exception, negative thought dwelling always preceeds negative feelings. If I eliminate my negative thought dwelling, I eliminate my negative feelings.

Being wise means persistently exercising self-discipline to draw upon the God Power Who dwells within me to perpetually control my thought dwelling.

When we exercise this self-control and self-discipline, we are always victorious in overpowering Satan-I. The Bible is replete with references to this Divine Power, and how it should be used by the wise man and woman:

Sin is a demon lurking at the door; his urge is toward you, yet you can be his master. (Gen. 4:7 NAB)

A wise man has great power, and a man of knowledge increases strength. (Prov. 24:5 NIV)

Finally, be strong in the Lord and in his mighty power (God-I). Put on the full armor of God so that you can take your stand against the devil's schemes (Satan-I). (Eph. 6:10–11 NIV)

It is also clear that once we put on the armor of God and *habitually* kill all our Satan-I negative thoughts, and only dwell upon our God-I positive thoughts, Satan will flee from us. Like Mother Teresa, we will no longer be consumed with negative thought dwelling, which results in experiencing negative feelings. We will then be free to do God's work, as did Mother Teresa.

Submit yourselves, then, to God (God-I). Resist the devil (Satan-I) and he will flee from you. Come near to God and he will come near to you. (Choosing-I and God-I uniting.) (James 4:7 NIV)

God has empowered us to thrash Satan-I and to live a life filled with enduring peace of mind. To live a Spirit filled life, the type of life God wants us to live, we must learn how to *habitually* only dwell upon God-I positive thoughts and habitually obliterate Satan-I negative thoughts. When we do that, we live by the Spirit and we reject the flesh.

Before I introduce you to the all-important methodology of controlling your thought dwelling, let us review the basics.

Say to yourself:
1. I have no control over what God-I or Satan-I thoughts spontaneously enter my mind.
2. Of the thoughts that enter my mind, Choosing-I holds the tremendous power to choose which thought I accept and which thought I reject.
3. Once accepted, I alone am responsible for how long I dwell upon any thought that has been accepted by Choosing-I.
4. The longer I dwell upon positive thoughts, the more positive I feel. The longer I dwell upon negative thoughts, the more negative I feel.

Some examples:
Satan-I implants in your mind thoughts that you should never forgive the person who sexually or physically abused you as a child. That type of thought dwelling will certainly destroy your enduring peace of mind. God-I implants in your mind thoughts that you must forgive that person and get on with your life. God-I reminds you of what we say in the Lord's prayer, "Forgive us our trespasses as we forgive those who trespass against us." If you forgive, that will enhance your enduring peace of mind.

Satan-I implants in your mind thoughts of that stupid, stupid thing you did awhile ago. God-I implants in your mind thoughts that God has forgiven you and commands you to forgive yourself.

Satan-I implants in your mind thoughts of your handicap or illness. God-I implants in your mind thoughts of handicapped and ill people who transcended their physical limitations and lived full and rich lives. They did it. You can do it. That should give you incredible hope.

In each of those scenarios, Choosing-I determines which of those two type thoughts you dwell upon, and for how long you dwell upon any given thought.

What do we do about this battle that is constantly waging in our minds? How can we win? Do we have to go through life haphazardly when it comes to controlling thought dwelling? Isn't there some methodology by which we can once and for all control our thought dwelling, and therefore our feelings? In the final analysis, can we train Choosing-I to *habitually* do the correct thing when it comes to controlling our thought dwelling so that we can forever possess enduring peace of mind?

SOAP

Welcome to the most wonderful and exciting world of Stop, Obliterate, Alter, Praise! (SOAP). Say it over a few times. Stop, Obliterate, Alter, Praise. SOAP is the methodology by which we keep our minds squeaky-clean from all Satan-I self-defeating, negative thoughts. SOAP is absolutely indispensable if you hope to make peace with your past. Without SOAP, you can never have the feeling and security of enduring peace of mind. You will never be able to enjoy God's peace.

SOAP deals with the first Good Life Truth you met in this chapter, namely:

> I have absolutely no control over past events. They are dead and gone forever. However, I have absolute control over how

long I dwell upon negative thoughts about past events and the negative feelings that flow therefrom.

SOAP provides you with the unfailing and absolute ability to control how long you dwell upon negative thoughts about past events. Therefore, it is by using SOAP to control our thought dwelling that we control our feelings.

When we are beset with a Satan-I negative thought about an event from our past, we have two choices: Submit or act. If we submit, we dwell upon the Satan-I negative thought, which produces a Satan-I negative feeling. As Shakespeare said of submitting to evil, "O calm, dishonorable, vile submission!"

The only reasonable choice is to act. And that is what SOAP is about.

Let us discuss the powerful cleansing power of SOAP.

Stop

Whenever you become aware that you are entertaining a Satan-I negative, self-defeating thought *about anything*, you must yell, "Stop! Stop! Stop!" (Please be discrete. If you're in a crowd, yell it to yourself.)

Then you mercilessly attack your Satan-I thought. First, you recognize and address Satan-I. Say, "Satan-I, you really want me to dwell upon this self-defeating thought, don't you? Well-you-go-straight-to-hell! Be gone you despicable monster! Out-of-here! I am clothed with the armor and Power of God within me! *I can do all things through Him who gives me strength!*"

This is a matter about which you must not be timid. Satan is not timid with you. If you give him the opportunity he will chew you up and spit you out! Every time you begin to dwell upon a Satan-I negative thought, you *must* cry out, "Satan-I, be-out-of-here! Go-to-hell!"

I recently gave the Stop, Obliterate, Alter, Praise speech to the Merced Central Presbyterian Church Women's Club. Some of the older ladies were reticent about ordering Satan to "Go-to-hell!"

Fortunately, their Pastor was present and he assured them it was quite proper to utter such an exclamation. Although somewhat reluctant, they eventually got into the swing of SOAP, including telling Satan to "Go-to-hell!"

Obliterate

Then you proceed to Obliterate the negative thought. Viciously draw upon the Power that is the Holy Spirit within you! It is only by the Power of God within you that allows SOAP to work.

I like stabbing. I stab, stab, stab the thought until it is dead, dead, dead!

I must tell you, I receive *tremendous* pleasure in killing my Satan-I negative thoughts! I revel in the divine Power God gives me to totally crush Satan-I. I stab and stab and stab. It produces a real high. I prove over and over again that, if called upon, God Who is all-powerful, allows *me* to control how long I dwell upon any Satan-I negative thought that enters my mind. It is truly a case of "Ask and ye shall receive." Ask for the greatest Power in the universe to give you self-discipline over controlling the type of thoughts you dwell upon, and you shall receive it. Every time!

You will find that Obliterating Satan-I negative thoughts produces a great pleasure, a most exhilarating feeling. You will very much enjoy this process, this taking complete control of your thought dwelling. *It is exquisitely empowering!*

Alter

Now, Alter. With the Satan-I negative thought lying dead at my feet, sometimes I gleefully spit on it once or twice, I then replace it with a God-I pleasing or a neutral thought.

Let me distinguish between a pleasing and a neutral thought.

I keep on call a long series of God-I pleasing thoughts to replace a just killed Satan-I negative thought. I think about pleasant experiences with Eileen and/or our children and grandchildren. I think of all the wonderful holidays and vacations we've spent together. I think about scenic motorcycle rides with cousins and friends. Being a handyman, I think about the barbecue I built in our backyard, wainscoating our hallways, stairway and master bedroom, the game room I am still working on, and many other home projects. I think about hikes in the magnificent Sierra Nevada Mountains with my dear friend Bob McKenzie. I think about the mountain home that I will have some day. Sometime I just think about all God has given me. It is easy to maintain a portfolio of God-I pleasing thoughts.

If for some reason I cannot sustain a God-I pleasing thought, I elect to use a neutral thought. I then Alter the dead Satan-I thought with a thought about what I am going to cook for our next Gourmet Club meal. (I love to cook, especially with my dear friends Mike and Jeanne Salvadori.) When am I going to change the oil in Eileen's car or my pick-up? What about a case I am working on? And so on.

I encourage you to first attempt to Alter with a pleasant memory. We all have enough pleasant memories to last us a lifetime. Think of the good things you have experienced. Make a list of all the blessings in your life, and the good things you believe the future holds for you. Write down all the obstacles you met head on and conquered. You'll be surprised at the abundance of pleasant memories in your memory bank. Dig them out. You will enjoy not only the result, but the process as well. That becomes your Alter list. Keep it handy. Use it. It will keep you feeling content.

Jesus eloquently sets forth the great danger when we kill a Satan-I negative thought, but fail to replace it with a God-I positive or neutral thought.

> When an unclean spirit [Satan-I] goes out of a man, he goes through dry places, seeking rest; and finding none, he says, "I will return to my house from which I came." And when he comes, he finds it swept and put in order. Then he goes and takes with him seven other spirits more wicked than himself, and they en-

ter and dwell there; and the last state of that man is worse than the first. (Luke 11:24 NKJV)

If after Obliterating we fail to Alter, seven more Satan-I thoughts move in and our last state of mind is worse than our first.

Praise

In this final step you will either healthily Praise yourself or Praise God, depending on the type of Satan-I negative thought you have just Stopped, Obliterated, and Altered.

Most Satan-I negative thoughts are self-defeating. They make you feel worthless, ashamed, embarrassed, humiliated, discouraged, disgusted, or disgraced. You feel stupid and you hate yourself when you dwell upon one of these Satan-I negative thoughts.

But you know you are not a worthless, stupid, or hateful person. Therefore, it is imperative that after Stopping, Obliterating, and Altering, you take a big dose of *healthy* self-praise. Slowly say to yourself something like:

- I am a good person.
- I have much self-worth.
- I am loved by many relatives and friends.
- I am a good husband/wife, parent/child.
- I am a kind person.
- I am a nice person.
- I have provided well for my family.
- I do my job well. I am a hard worker.
- I love many people and many people love me.
- I bring sunshine into the lives of many people.
- I do many charitable works.
- I help the needy whenever I encounter them.
- I am valuable.
- It is good to be alive.
- I am a precious child of God.

Create your own praise litany, but create and use it *now*.

There are those occasions when you may feel that praising yourself is not necessary and would be inappropriate. The Satan-I negative thought you just killed did not make you feel worthless, ashamed, embarrassed, humiliated, disgraced, stupid, or hate yourself. It is the type of Satan-I thought that made you feel sad that things are the way they are through no fault of your own. For example, the deplorable condition of our once great nation and the world in general. This is a very disagreeable thought and one Satan-I uses over and over again to lead us to despair and to stop having faith in God. In those situations, after you have Stopped, Obliterated, and Altered, then Praise God.

- Blessed be God!
- Blessed be His Holy Name!
- Thank You God for all You have given me.
- Forgive me for losing faith in Your Almighty Power.
- Forgive me for losing faith in Your ability to assist me if only I ask.
- Thank You for SOAP to rid myself of these Satan-I negative thoughts.
- Let me focus on the beauty of this present moment.
- Come God-I, fill my heart with peace.

Once you master the skill of *habitually* using Stop, Obliterate, Alter, Praise, it will take you only a few seconds to eradicate each Satan-I negative thought as it enters your mind.

In summary:

Stop! "Satan-I, you really want me to dwell upon this thought, don't you? Well-you-go-straight-to-hell! This is not an acceptable thought! *I can do all things through Him who gives me strength!*"

Obliterate! Stab. Stab. Stab. Stab.

Alter. That hike in the beautiful Sierra Nevada Mountains with my dear friend Bob McKenzie. What a great dessert I have planned for our next Gourmet Club meal.

Praise. "Blessed be God! Blessed be His Holy Name! I can't believe how fortunate I am to have all I possess. What a wonderful life this is! God truly blessed this Lebanese-Italian kid. Thank you God for giving me SOAP so I can have enduring peace of mind."

Occasionally, I experience a very persistent Satan-I self-defeating thought that cannot be eradicated with just one SOAPing. When this occurs, I chant a mantra of Stop, Obliterate, Alter, Praise; Stop, Obliterate, Alter, Praise; Stop, Obliterate, Alter, Praise.

Eventually, Satan-I retreats from the battlefield of my mind. I am again at peace. God and I win big time.

When you *habitually* use SOAP, two things simultaneously occur:

First, your Choosing-I and your God-I grow closer together. They will soon have you gently smiling. You feel contentment. You feel inner peace. You feel empowered. You know everything is going to be all right. You have regained your enduring peace of mind. Your God-I keeps feeding up more pleasant thoughts. You realize that thoughts about events from your past (or thoughts about the present or the future) can never hurt you again. You are empowered by the strength of the Holy Spirit within you.

How wonderful it would be if everyone in the world chose to rid themselves of their Satan-I negative thoughts by using SOAP. The results would be staggering.

Second, your Satan-I is in hiding. It is as if universal Satan recalled your Satan-I and sent him searching for another person who is unaware.

It is sad that many people are not aware of the concept, *I alone choose how long I dwell upon any thought which enters my mind,* nor of the concept of SOAPing away every Satan-I negative thought that comes into his or her mind. Unaware people dwell for long periods of time on self-defeating, Satan-I negative thoughts and are beset with negative feelings that flow from Satan-I stinking-thinking.

On the brighter side, I am amazed at how many people seem to intuitively understand SOAPing without ever being able to articulate it. We see people who regardless of their past or present circumstances exhibit contentment, inner peace, and enduring peace of mind. We very much admire them for their qualities. Without realizing it, they are masters at the SOAP methodology.

My mother was a first generation little Italian lady (4 feet-10 inches tall; in truth, she was a *giant!*). Although she could never have articulated it, my mother was a master at SOAP. I learned much about life from her.

Adeline Hider

My mother was the second of six children. She dropped out of high school after her sophomore year to begin working. That was necessary to provide additional income for her family. Although a high school dropout, she was extremely wise. My mother endlessly lived **Stop, Obliterate, Alter, Praise.** We children often went to her seeking pity because of some perceived transgression perpetrated upon us. We never got the pity we sought. Her stock observations were always the same: "Honey, if this is the worst thing that happens in your life, thank God." Or, "Honey, don't think about it, it's over and done." Or, her favorite, "Honey, always remember, life is what you make it."

She always brought everything clearly into perspective. We were taught to intuitively and habitually, banish every Satan-I thought that entered our minds. We were unknowingly taught SOAP. The hurt was always washed away. Life was very good growing up with my mother. She was *never* parked under a cherry tree.

The last conversation I had with my mother was when she was on her deathbed in Toledo, Ohio. Eileen and I were at the San Francisco Airport ready to board an airplane for Toledo. My mother had suffered for a long time. We knew she did not have long to live. I called to let her know we would soon be there.

I concluded our conversation with some silly words of encouragement. Something like, "Don't worry Mom, everything is going to be OK." The inept student trying to advise the wise master. Characteristically she replied, "Honey, I can't complain. I've had a very good life." We said goodbye for the last time.

Our plane stopped over in Atlanta, Georgia. I remember the airport seemed especially dark and dank. I called Toledo Hospital. My mother had gone home.(Ironically, I am writing this on Mother's Day. It is my last tangible gift to my mother. I share with you another of her favorite quotes: "God truly works in strange ways." He certainly does Mom.)

My mother had an endless supply of SOAP. Looking back, I realize that throughout all the years I had the pleasure of being with this marvelous woman, her puzzle was complete. But, then, I think it always was.

People like my mother are not immune from their Satan-I. They too have negative thoughts. However, they choose to never dwell upon these Satan-I negative thoughts. They know to Stop and Obliterate each negative thought at its inception. The dead thought is quickly Altered with a healthy, positive thought. And they never cease praising God.

Even as they pass through death to their new and glorious lives, they choose to think only about the good things that occurred during their earthly lives. They choose to only dwell upon their God-I positive thoughts. They continually affirm their self-worth. They intuitively know, *I alone choose how long I dwell upon any thought which enters my mind.* SOAPing gives them control of their thought dwelling. Knowing that their thoughts cause their feelings, they intuitively come to know, *I alone am responsible for how I feel every conscious moment of my life.* They are wise. We can make the same choice. We, too, can be wise.

We all know people like my mother. They will neither say a bad word nor do an evil deed, no matter what life hurls across their path. They live SOAP.

To the contrary, we all know people who almost never say anything good about anyone or seldom do a good deed for anyone.

What thoughts do you suppose they are killing? I wonder if the God-I within each of them ever gives up feeding them positive thoughts.

In my own case, my Choosing-I is blissfully aware that he has control over my thought selection and rejection. After many years of practicing SOAP, he *habitually* chooses to have me only dwell upon God-I positive thoughts. Why would he choose to have me dwell upon Satan-I negative thoughts of such things as my deadly prostate cancer, a radical prostatectomy, remaining cancer and daily radiation treatments, in lieu of God-I thinking about my wonderful extended family, friends, a glorious life here on earth, and the exciting expectation of an infinitely more glorious life hereafter? I would not.

You must not be foolish. No matter what happened in your past, you must not seek anyone else's pity. You do not need your own Satan-I self-pity. You most definitely must not feel worthless or powerless. You are not worthless or powerless. You are a good and worthy person. You have much value. You are God's magnificent creation. You have the tremendous Power of Almighty God at the center of your being. If you draw upon that Power, you are invincible!

If you don't intuitively use SOAP, you *must* overhaul your thinking process so that you *habitually* use SOAP every time a negative, self-defeating thought enters your mind. To get in the habit of using SOAP is nothing more than self-discipline. There is nothing you will ever do that will pay you a greater dividend than *habitually* using SOAP. Simply stated, if you ever hope to have *enduring* peace of mind, you must *habitually* use SOAP every time a Satan-I self-defeating thought enters your mind. *Every time!*

If you choose not to use SOAP and continue to dwell upon an internal list of Satan-I negative thoughts, you will continue to experience bad feelings. This only earthly life you have will seem disappointing and bad to you. You cannot enjoy inner peace, joy, contentment, or enduring peace of mind. You are wasting the precious present moment because of listening to Satan-I. You are letting what happened in one of your yesterdays destroy the peace of your today. That pleases Satan-I. It makes you unhappy. It is always your choice.

For your sake and well being, please make the correct choice. *Choose* to only dwell upon God-I positive thoughts. *Choose* to *habitually* SOAP away every Satan-I negative thought that enters your mind. That choice determines who you are, saint or sinner, contented or unhappy.

Be prepared! Stop, Obliterate, Alter, Praise is anathema to Satan. Satan-I is going to put up a hell of a battle when you commence using SOAP. For all your life, your Satan-I may have had his way with you, filling your mind with self-defeating, hating, loathsome thoughts about people, past events, and even yourself. And you foolishly *chose* to dwell upon such thoughts. That is going to be a difficult habit to break. But have no doubt, the habit can be broken the same way it was formed, one Satan-I thought at a time. You know it is your choice. *Choose* to send Satan-I negative thoughts straight to hell. *Choose* a new and glorious life. Stop, Obliterate, Alter, Praise!

God rewards you handsomely for mastering the SOAP technique. Once you are proficient at SOAP, you notice an immediate change in yourself. After killing Satan-I negative thinking over and over again, you will experience the most wonderful feeling of taking complete control of your thought life. I know this is true because my close friends and I experience this control.

I motivated a number of my friends to try SOAP. They obliged me. The results were overwhelming! They are now strong advocates of this methodology of *controlling their lives by controlling their thought dwelling.*

What is interesting is the instrument of death each uses for Obliterating any Satan-I negative thought. Butch Hughes, a very close friend and minor-league baseball coach, batters Satan-I thoughts with a baseball bat. Pastor Bill Stephens, a true soul mate, stomps and stomps and stomps Satan-I thoughts until there is nothing, nothing, nothing left of the negative thought. Julie Vitato, my young athlete comrade in God, puts on her spiked shoes, gets the Satan-I thought properly positioned behind her, and spikes, spikes,

SPIRITUAL HEALING – MAKING PEACE WITH YOUR PAST

spikes. After introducing her to SOAP, Julie gave me one of the greatest compliments I ever received. She said, "Thank you for giving my life back to me." Of course, I didn't. She and her God-I did it.

But, one of my favorite Obliterate stories is about an attorney friend of mine:

Ron Marks

Like many of my acquaintances, Ron heard about my writing this book. He graciously offered to read and critique the final draft. When we later met, he confessed he chortled when he read my assertion that by *habitually* using SOAP and Obliterating every Satan-I negative thought that comes into one's mind, a person will experience the feeling of being exquisitely empowered and can instantly take control of his or her thought dwelling. Well, the chortler is now a believer!

Ron's method of Obliterating is most interesting. He treats each negative self-defeating thought as a small Satan-I, a "devilette". He grabs his trusty baseball bat, throws the negative thought devilette into the air, and knocks it out of the ballpark of his mind.

Ron assures me that after habitually using SOAP for a short period of time, he was carefully searching through his mind seeking other devilettes to Obliterate, all to no avail! He felt a glow and experienced a powerful white light. In his words, as a result of using SOAP, "It also becomes abundantly clear how much better we feel once we are able to stop obsessing on negative thoughts and move onto happier, nobler thoughts." How's that for a testimony?!

Are you sick and tired of "obsessing on negative thoughts"? Do you want to "move onto happier, nobler thoughts"? Then start SOAPing! Select your favorite instrument for Obliterating Satan-I negative thoughts, but get on with it!

A Word of Caution

I do not want to be misunderstood. I am not remotely suggesting that with the use of SOAP you are going to feel euphoric, really happy, happy, happy all the time. It is not rational to expect to continually feel this way. There is a tremendous difference between the euphoric and *transitory* feeling of happiness and the deep-seated and *constant* feeling of enduring peace of mind. No one can show you how to be happy ever moment of your life. But God has shown us how to have contentment and enduring peace of mind every moment of our lives. To have uninterrupted and enduring contentment with frequent periods of happiness is all we can hope for in this life. That is certainly more than most people experience. As for total happiness, it is reserved for the next life.

So, be prepared. At times, you will experience the "Dark Night of the Soul," as discussed by Saint John of the Cross. God allows that so we stay close to Him. However, no matter how dark the night, by using SOAP, you will not feel down, anxious, or unhappy. You remain stoic and strong in God's faithfulness that you will overcome those doldrums, those feelings of sullenness or moodiness. Those feelings are as ephemeral as a wisp of smoke. You know they will soon pass away. As Edward Young, the English poet stated, "'Tis impious in a good man to be sad."

You should never be sad. You have the security of knowing you have more than you will ever need of God's Power within you to defeat Satan, no matter what he throws at you. You come to trust and rely on that Power within you. I assure you, it will *never* fail you.

Once again, I am compelled to stress that nowhere is habit more important than in controlling thought dwelling. Until you *habitually* practice SOAP, you cannot have the good life. Every time you have a Satan-I negative thought, you must say, "Get thee behind me Satan. Go-straight-to-hell! I'm not going to let you destroy my enduring peace of mind," and then Obliterate, Alter, Praise. Until you *habitually* do that, you have no hope of ever completing your puzzle.

The question is not *whether* you are responsible for how long you dwell upon any self-defeating, negative thought. Clearly, you are. The question is *will* you acknowledge this responsibility and do something about it? Will you *habitually* SOAP away every Satan-I self-defeating negative thought that enters your mind? Or, will you dwell upon the Satan-I negative thoughts that enter your mind and suffer the negative feelings that flow therefrom? It is your choice.

When it comes to enduring peace of mind, the most important decision you will ever make is whether you will take complete control of your thought dwelling. That decision will determine what kind of life you have. In the extremes, you can be a Mother Teresa or an Adolf Hitler. The choice is yours. I pray that you choose wisely.

Postscript

In this book, we utilize the SOAP methodology to Obliterate all Satan-I negative thoughts about past events. Unless we do that, we will never make peace with our respective pasts.

However, you are very wise if you utilize the SOAP methodology to deal with *any* self-defeating thought, whether it concerns your past, present, or future.

Self-defeating thoughts take on an entirely different meaning when we discuss them in the context of your present and your future. For example, there is good and bad daydreaming. You should indulge in good daydreaming, something which will revolutionize the computer industry. You should Obliterate bad day-dreaming; it is a tremendous waste of the awesome present moment. As my attorney friend Ron Marks says, "With respect to compulsive thoughts that may be disguised as pleasant thoughts, I can give a couple of examples. People may have compulsive thoughts about achieving economic security through making and investing money. Those compulsive thoughts may go way beyond what is prudent and necessary to get them through life. In connection with achieving financial success, they may daydream excessively about winning the Lotto, winnings from gambling, or making a fortune in business. I believe that those types of thoughts can be just as negative as the thoughts of people who dwell upon past events that may have hurt them or past events where they may have hurt someone else." I totally agree with that assessment.

Likewise, any thought that causes you anxiety or fear about the future should be mercilessly Obliterated.

God has given you the all-powerful sword of SOAP to defeat Satan-I thoughts about your past, present, or future. For your mental well-being, learn well how to use this mighty weapon.

Synopsis

Say to yourself:

I experience God-I positive and Satan-I negative thoughts. I know the type of thought I dwell upon determines how I feel. Since I do not want to feel negative, I would be foolish to dwell upon negative thoughts, especially negative thoughts about my past. Therefore, I must forever cease to dwell upon Satan-I negative thoughts about my past. I cease to dwell upon such thoughts by *habitually* SOAPing away negative thoughts whenever they come into my mind. This does not mean I sweep all thoughts of past trauma under the rug. If I do, I will never be healed. I must only think about past trauma in terms of God-I positive thoughts. Once I learn this technique, I will make peace with my past. I will then enjoy immutable enduring peace of mind.

GOOD LIFE TRUTHS
DERIVED FROM CHAPTER FOUR

4-1.   I have absolutely no control over past events. They are dead and gone forever. However, I have absolute control over how long I dwell upon negative thoughts about past events and the negative feelings that flow therefrom.

4-2.   Without exception, negative thought dwelling always precedes negative feelings. If I eliminate my negative thought dwelling, I eliminate my negative feelings.

4-3.   Being wise means persistently exercising self-discipline to draw upon the God Power Who dwells within me to perpetually control my thought dwelling.

4-4.   Stop, Obliterate, Alter, Praise, is the only methodology that gives me complete control of my thought dwellng.

4-5.   To make peace with my past, I must *habitually* SOAP away Satan-I negative thinking about my past. There can never be an exception to this rule. Never!.

PART THREE

UNDERSTANDING THE NATURE OF THE PAST

CHAPTER FIVE

THE PAST DOES NOT EXIST

A word of caution; in these three brief chapters, which deal with the nature of the past, you will find no tools such as SOAP, or Healing Steps as provided in the next section of the book. However, do not discount the importance of these chapters. They are an essential foundation for what lies ahead. Each chapter carries a powerful truth about *the past*, which you must internalize if you are to come to peace with your past. The importance of understanding the actual nature of *the past* cannot be overstated. Only by understanding the nature of *the past*, can you come to peace with your past.

There are four significant characteristics of *the past* that should create for you a new, fresh, and exciting way in which you think about your past:

1. There is no such thing as *the past* (this chapter).
2. Your past no longer exists, except in your memory (this chapter).
3. Your past can never be changed (Chapter Six).
4. Past events are feelingless (Chapter Seven).

There Is No Such Thing As *the Past*

Let me begin with a bold assertion. Except in the mind of God, where it is the present, there is no such thing as *the past*. You probably do not believe that, but it is true. Because of our sloppy language, we often say things we know are not true, as an example, sunrise and sunset. The sun does not rise. The sun does not set. It just appears that way.

So it is with *the past*. We are accustomed to talking about *the past* as if our ancestors, our progeny, and we all share in the same past, or some cumulative past, and as if it really continues to exist at the present moment. Neither of those propositions is true.

If there were such a thing as *the past*, meaning a common past for all of us, you would remember the building of the pyramids and many of my high school classmates. I would remember the building of the acropolis and many of your high school classmates. But you do not and I do not. Your past is your past. My past is my past. No two human beings in the history of the world ever had exactly the same past. Nor will it ever occur. The past for each of us is as unique to us as is our DNA and fingerprints.

Of course, there are past events of such magnitude that when they occurred they became part of many people's pasts. These events include World Wars I and II, the Korean War, the Vietnam War, the Middle East Wars, the assassination of world leaders, economic depressions, etc. But, unless you were there, those are nothing more than past events you somehow learned about. Unless you were there, they are really not part of *your* past. In the final analysis, everything that has occurred since God created the universe is nothing more than a chronological series of past events. A few happened in your and my pasts. Most did not.

Concerning tangible things, although they had their origins in past times, they do not exist in the past. Clearly, they exist only in the present.

When and if we begin to speak more explicitly, we will no longer speak of *the past*. Instead, we will speak of your past, my past, and past events.

I encourage you to accept your past as *your past*. It is your past life. It doesn't belong to anyone else, only you. Once you do this, you can take possession of all the events of your past life. When you take possession of all the events of your past life, you can handle them, see them, hear them, and most importantly, you can then fix the thoughts of those past experiences that need to be fixed. You can truly make past events historical only, without debilitating emotions in the present moment, as we shall see.

Your Past Does Not Exist, Except in Your Memory

When dealing with your past, you must realize it does not exist, except in your memory.

What happened to you twenty years ago, one year ago, one day ago or even one second ago is gone forever. It no longer exists anywhere in this world, except in your memory. There is no place on earth where you can go to visit your past. The only place you and I can be, or can visit, is the present moment.

If it were not for memory, there would be no past. Without memory, there is only the present. For amoeba, bacteria, and earthworms, which have no memory, there is no past. In that one sense, they are more fortunate than we are since they have no unpleasant memories of past events to upset them in the present moment. They have no emotional baggage. But few of us would change places with them, which leads us to our first Good Life Truth for this chapter:

> The events that occurred in my past are gone forever. All that remains in the present moment are my memories of nonexistent past events. Therefore, my past does not exist, except in my memory.

It should be intuitively obvious that if your past does not exist, except in your memory, past events cannot possibly hurt you in the present moment. The only things that can hurt you are your internal, secret, present personal thoughts about past events. Therefore, please realize and accept the fact that a nonexistent past event, in and of itself, can never again hurt you. That includes the sexual molestation, the bitter divorce, the shame to which you were put, your spouse's extramarital affair, your own indiscretions, alcoholism, substance abuse, and your own stupid blunders. Only by negative thinking is it possible for a nonexistent past event to hurt you in the present moment.

Which brings us to two more Good Life Truths:

Since my memory alone holds my past, and I can deal with my memory, then I can deal with my past.

Events from my past cannot hurt me. Only Satan-I negative stinking-thinking about a past event can hurt me. Knowing that, I will habitually and vigorously SOAP away every Satan-I negative thought about a past event.

Then, you ask, "If those nonexistent past events no longer exist, and can't hurt me in the present moment, how come I hurt so badly?!"

You hurt so badly because you allow yourself to dwell upon Satan-I self-defeating, negative thoughts about nonexistent past events. It is not nonexistent past events that hurt you. It is how you *think* about nonexistent past events that hurt you. People and events cannot permanently hurt us. Only our Satan-I negative thinking about past events can permanently hurt us.

To our detriment, we choose to dwell in the present moment on negative thoughts about past events that no longer exist. And, Satan loves it!

To come to peace with your past and to stop hurting yourself, it is imperative that you immediately cease dwelling upon self-defeating thoughts of nonexistent past events. And you stop dwelling upon those self-defeating thoughts of nonexistent past events by *habitually* SOAPing them away the very instant Satan-I raises such a thought in your mind.

However, I once again stress that I am not remotely suggesting that you attempt to sweep *all* thoughts of those events from your mind. Not only would it be impossible to do so, but God wants to work a miracle in your life. God *wants* you to think about and deal with the thoughts of those nonexistent past events in a particular way we soon will discuss in great detail.

Therefore, please keep the next two Good Life Truths indelibly etched in you mind:

I must never attempt to Obliterate all thoughts of a nonexistent past event. If I do so, I will never make peace with my past.

Correctly thinking about nonexistent past events can be very valuable to me and can lead to gainful insight about myself.

Immense knowledge and wisdom can be learned from reflecting upon our own or other people's past experiences. We often learn more from mistakes than from successes. Mistake can present a valuable learning experience. Correctly thinking about nonexistent past events can lead to gainful insight about one's self. Correct thinking allows us to reflect upon and analyze the bad choices we made and why we made them. Without reflection, we have difficulty in breaking a destructive habit. In that sense, reflecting upon nonexistent past events is good and highly beneficial.

What I propose is that if your thought of any past event is self-defeating, causes you to be upset and angry, and has no positive benefit to you, then you must immediately Stop, Obliterate, Alter, Praise it away. It is only when you can think of that event in a learning manner that you should dwell upon it.

George Santayana, an American philosopher, was correct when he stated, "Those who cannot remember the past are condemned to repeat it." That applies to both a personal and a national history. Socrates was also correct when he stated, "The unexamined life is not worth living." However, the old adage is true, "There is no use crying over spilt milk." And the Bible tells us:

> Brothers, I do not consider myself yet to have taken hold of it. But one thing I do: *Forgetting what is behind* and straining toward what is ahead, I press on toward the goal to win the prize for which God has called me heavenward in Christ Jesus. *All of us who are mature should take such a view of things. . . .* (Phil. 3:13–15 NIV)

It is certainly clear that St. Paul never cried over spilt milk, "Forgetting what is behind and straining toward what is ahead." Although seemingly so, the various concepts concerning examining one's life and forgetting what is behind are not inconsistent, as we shall see.

Synopsis

Say to yourself:

I understand that it is impossible for two people to have the same past. I accept the fact that my past is as unique to me as my DNA and fingerprints. I also understand that past events that occurred in my life no longer exist anywhere in the universe. Only thoughts of my past exist, and they exist only in my memory. When I accept these truths, I realize that my memory alone holds my past. I can deal with my memory. Therefore, I can deal with my past. Knowing that, I am well on the road to eliminating emotionally disturbing thoughts about nonexistent past events. I am well on my way to coming to peace with my past. Wow, that's exciting!

GOOD LIFE TRUTHS
DERIVED FROM CHAPTER FIVE

5-1.   The events that occurred in my past are gone forever. All that remains in the present moment are my memories of nonexistent past events. Therefore, my past does not exist, except in my memory.

5-2.   Since my memory alone holds my past, and I can deal with my memory, then I can deal with my past.

5-3.   Events from my past cannot hurt me. Only Satan-I negative stinking-thinking about a past event can hurt me. Knowing that, I will habitually and vigorously SOAP away every Satan-I negative thought about a past event.

5-4.   I must never attempt to Obliterate *all* thoughts of a nonexistent past event. If I do so, I will never make peace with my past.

5-5.   Correctly thinking about nonexistent past events can be very valuable to me and can lead to gainful insight about myself.

CHAPTER SIX

ONE'S PAST CAN NEVER BE CHANGED

Exhibitionist Shane

Shane is a professional in our community. He is also an exhibitionist. The first time the police apprehended Shane in the act of exhibiting himself, he had no criminal record. Because of no record, his attorney was able to negotiate a plea bargain with the District Attorney whereby Shane would spend no time in jail. He was placed on probation and given a considerable period of community service.

Unfortunately for Shane, he reoffended. Because of violating his probation, Shane was given a jail sentence and reinstated on probation for three years. Shane almost lost his professional license. Needless to say, Shane became the talk of the town. It was rumored he was going to take his family and move away from Merced. However, they never did relocate.

Shane and I occasionally discuss his plight. That is, if you call this a discussion, "How could I be so stupid? How could I be so stupid? I can't believe I'm so stupid!" (More later about not being able to separate who we are from what we did.)

People close to Shane tell me that thoughts of his shameful acts totally preoccupy him. He would give or do almost anything to undo those past acts. Of course, there is absolutely nothing he can do to change his transgressions or his past.

The same shackles restrain all of us.

If you were as rich as the Rockefellers, Gettys, Kennedys, Bill Gates, and every other wealthy family in the world combined, you could not change by one iota a detail of an event from your past.

If you possessed the amalgamated power of every air force, navy, and army that ever marched the face of the earth, you could not change one speck of a detail of an event from your past.

If you were as famous as the composite of Marilyn Monroe, the Beatles, Michael Jackson, and Michael Jordan, you could not change one scintilla of a detail of an event from your past.

No matter how rich, powerful, or famous you are, it doesn't matter. You cannot change any of your past one splinter. Your past is immutable. What has happened, has happened. What was, was, and shall be forever more.

The spousal beating, sexual molestation or abuse, the bitter divorce, the loss of a child, the betrayal by your dearest friend, substance abuse, alcoholism, the most stupid thing you ever did, can never be changed a smidgen.

In the form of two Good Life Truths, that concept becomes:

> No matter how rich, powerful, or famous I am, I cannot change by one splinter an event from my past. What has happened, has happened. What was, was, and will be forever more. It's over. It's done forever.

> I must unequivocally accept the fact that every past event in my life is unchangeable.

Wise people realize that what occurred in the unchangeable past, occurred in the unchangeable past. It is forever done. How we each feel in the present moment is how we each feel in the present moment. Our feelings are now.

Unless we allow it, what occurred in our unchangeable past has absolutely nothing to do with how we feel in the present moment. How we feel in the present moment is determined by what thoughts we choose to dwell upon about our unchangeable past.

Extrapolating from an earlier Good Life Truth, *I have absolutely no control over past events. They are dead and gone forever. However, I have absolute control over how long I dwell upon negative thoughts about past events and the feelings that flow therefrom*, we derive a new Good Life Truth:

> I realize it is not unchangeable past events that cause me discontentment. It is choosing to dwell upon Satan-I negative thoughts about unchangeable past events that causes me discontentment.

One must become wise to make peace with one's past. As we become wise, we accept that we alone determine how a past unchangeable event affects our present moment peace of mind. We learn from people like Luminary Mary and Adeline Hider that we don't have to let the memory of an unchangeable past event destroy our present moment peace of mind. We remind ourselves of a Good Life Truth from Chapter One: *I must never let what happened in one of my yesterdays destroy the peace of my today*.

Your Satan-I tells you differently, hoping to get you to dwell upon self-defeating negative thoughts of an immutable past event. But, your Satan-I has a vested interest. Your Satan-I will do *anything* to take over your mind. At all costs, you must prevent this! If Satan can induce you to indulge in negative thinking about an unchangeable past event, he has the opportunity to destroy your enduring peace of mind in this world, and ultimately to possess your soul in hell.

Which leads us to:

> I must never again dwell upon Satan-I self-defeating thoughts of wishing I could change anything from my past. Instead, I must change how I think about unchangeable past events.

I must learn how to think about unchangeable past events only in God-I positive thoughts. Therein lies God's peace. When I learn how to do that, thoughts of my unchangeable past will never again destroy my present moment peace of mind.

We know there is absolutely nothing we can do to change a single speck of one's past. Then why do people dwell upon thoughts of an unchangeable past event and irrationally and hopelessly yearn to change it? Why do people think about an unchangeable past event over and over again, foolishly wishing it had never occurred? Why are people like Exhibitionist Shane? The answers are the same: Satan-I. And what a tremendous waste of our valuable, but limited energy to wish we could change our pasts. Satan-I loves it when we indulge in such foolish thought dwelling.

If we stop *subjectively* blaming an unchangeable past event for how we feel in the present moment, through God's magnificent grace, we can grow closer to God-I and closer to peace. At least intellectually accept the fact that every past event is unchangeable. Say it to yourself, *I unequivocally accept the fact that every past event is unchangeable*. Repeat that proposition until it is indelible in your mind.

Of course, that does not mean there is no hope. Quite the contrary. It is enormous intellectual growth to realize that even though a past event is unchangeable, how we think about that past event is quite changeable. We don't dwell upon thoughts of wishing that past events could be changed. Instead, we change the way we think about unchangeable past events. We reject Satan-I negative thought dwelling when we think about the past event. We learn to put things into proper perspective. That is precisely how one makes peace with one's past. That changed method of thinking raises us to a higher level of consciousness.

Although seemingly trite, the old adage, "There's no use crying over split milk," is especially apropos in this discussion.

Whether it is something really stupid you did in your past or something terrible someone or Fate did to you, it can never be changed. You must accept that fact.

Synopsis

Say to yourself:

Satan-I implants in my mind the strongest desire to want to change events from my past. 'Oh, how I wish I never did that! How could I have been so stupid! I'd give anything if that never happened to me!' I will not be hoodwinked by Satan-I. I know my past, from the moment of my conception to one second ago, is entirely unchangeable. No matter how desperately I might wish it, no past event can ever be changed or undone. I unequivocally accept the fact that I can never change one detail of any past event. However, that should not lead me to despair since I now realize it is not unchangeable past events that cause me discontentment. It is choosing to think about unchangeable past events in an erroneous manner that causes me discontentment. I must learn how to think about unchangeable past events only in God-I positive thoughts. Therein lies God's peace. When I learn how to do that, thoughts of unchangeable past events will never again destroy my present moment peace of mind. I am liberated by the prospect that I have total freedom to change the way I think about unchangeable past events!

GOOD LIFE TRUTHS
DERIVED FROM CHAPTER SIX

6-1.   No matter how rich, powerful, or famous I am, I cannot change by one splinter an event from my past. What has happened, has happened. What was, was, and will be forever more. It's over. It's done forever.

6-2.   I must unequivocally accept the fact that every past event in my life is unchangeable.

6-3.   I realize it is not unchangeable past events that cause me discontentment. It is choosing to dwell upon Satan-I negative thoughts about unchangeable past events that causes me discontentment.

6-4.   I must never again dwell upon Satan-I self-defeating thoughts of wishing I could change anything from my past. Instead, I must change how I think about unchangeable past events.

6-5.   I must learn how to think about unchangeable past events only in God-I positive thoughts. Therein lies God's peace. When I learn how to do that, thoughts of my unchangeable past will never again destroy my present moment peace of mind.

CHAPTER SEVEN

PAST EVENTS
ARE FEELINGLESS

Do not be too hasty to answer the following questions:

1. When a world leader is assassinated, does it make you feel good or bad?
2. When someone commits suicide, does it make you feel good or bad?
3. When you learn someone is terminally ill with cancer, does it make you feel good or bad?
4. When a hurricane destroys crops worth millions of dollars, does it make you feel good or bad?
5. Do all child molestations cause bad feelings?

The answer to each of these questions is a resounding, "It all depends."

In this chapter we will confirm that past events cause us no feelings in and of themselves. Past events are past events. That's all they are. They are nothing more. They are nothing less. They can never be anything more or less than feelingless past events.

It is our relationship to the feelingless past event that causes us to have a positive or negative feeling when we think about the past event.

Let's return to our questions.

1. *When a world leader is assassinated, does it make you feel good or bad?*

Obviously, it depends on your relationship to the world leader.

When President John Fitzgerald Kennedy was assassinated on November 22, 1963, most people were severely grief stricken. But not everyone was. Assuming Lee Harvey Oswald assassinated JFK, he most probably was quite elated with his success.

It is no secret JFK had many fierce enemies. There can be little doubt that they were overjoyed when they heard of the President's demise.

It is evident that the assassination of JFK had no feelings in and of itself. His assassination is just another past event in the continuum of time. Whether you loved, admired, or hated the man determines your feelings about his assassination.

I suspect present-day teenagers have neither strong good nor bad feelings when they contemplate JFK's assassination. To them, it is a remote past event about which they know very little. When they hear the story, it causes minimal or no emotional impact. This substantiates the point. The assassination of a world leader is feelingless. Each of us gives his or her own feelings to any past event.

2. *When someone commits suicide, does it make you feel good or bad?*

You know the answer. It depends on your relationship to the deceased.

During World War II, Adolph Hitler was responsible for establishing ghastly concentration camps and causing the commission of bloodcurdling atrocities therein. He was single-handedly responsible for the horrible deaths of millions of innocent men, women, and children. He was intensely loathed by most of the civilized world. The free-world multitudes clamored unceasingly for his death.

When Adolf Hitler snuffed out his life in the now famous bunker, it sent the Allies into explosive jubilation. His self-induced death signaled total and triumphant victory by the Allies over the Nazis. It meant the end of the War in Europe. It was a truly blessed event. Or, was it?

Can you imagine the personal devastation if you were a high commander in the Third Reich? Should you follow der Fuhrer's path? Should you surrender to the hated Americans or the more hated Soviets? Should you attempt to flee to Brazil or some other foreign country?

At the time, there were intense good and bad feelings generated by Hitler's suicide. And what happened to those incredibly intense feelings felt by both sides when they learned of Hitler's death? Unlike the 1940's, it would now be difficult to find many people who give much thought to Hitler. Except in the recollections of persons directly affected by that demon, memory of his heinous deeds has substantially vanished. Hitler has slipped to the lowly level of being nothing more than an historical loser. For most people who were alive during World War II and are still alive, highly emotionally disturbing thoughts of his deeds have dulled and become little more than historical events.

Obviously, anyone's suicide, in and of itself, is a feelingless event.

3. *When you learn someone is terminally ill, does it make you feel good or bad?*

You feel one way if it is one of your loving parents. You feel quite the opposite if you are an Ally and it is an Adolf Hitler or Joseph Stalin. Someone being terminally ill is a phenomenon that has absolutely no feeling in and of itself.

4. *When a hurricane destroys food crops worth millions of dollars, do you feel good or bad about it?*

If you are the farmer whose crop is ravaged, depending on your net worth, it could mean the loss of everything you own. To a mentally unstable farmer, through Satan-I's influence, it could mean suicide. For those people interested in feeding the world population, it is a catastrophe.

On the other hand, a farmer halfway around the world from the hurricane may now get top dollar for his competing crop, which he desperately needs to avoid a bank foreclosure on his farm. It is going to be difficult for him to feel bad on payday.

Obviously, the event itself is feelingless. It is your relationship to the event that causes your feelings. But, you knew that.

5. *Do all child molestations create bad feelings?*
Let Matilda answer that question.

Molesting Matilda

Matilda is probably a nymphomaniac. She has a morbid and apparently uncontrollable sex drive. She especially likes young boys. (Although it is believed she also molested a few young girls.) I have no idea how many boys Matilda sexually molested. I do know I gave her the maximum possible prison term.

The probation officer interviewed the boys Matilda molested. Many are disturbed. Some are in therapy. Many of the boys dealt with their molestation and moved on with their lives. Of course, some of the boys were willing participants and quite enjoyed the experience. Although only teenagers, to them it was not a molestation.

As for Matilda, by studying her demeanor while in my courtroom, there is little doubt in my mind that she does not in the least regret her exploitations, even at the price of going to prison. After sternly handing down my lengthy sentence, with a wry smile on her face, Matilda's only comment was, "Judge Hider, you've got to do what you've got to do."

It was apparent to me that recollecting those molestations made her feel good.

It is undeniable that sexual molestation, in and of itself, is a feelingless event. It is what the participants think about those events that produce the resulting good or bad feelings.

You alone give feelings to the feelingless events of your past life. That is true regardless of what someone did to you, what Fate did to you, or that very stupid thing you did.

Synopsis

Say to yourself:

Past events in my life are just past events in my life. That's all they are. They are nothing more than feelingless events that occurred sometime in my past. My positive or negative feeling about a past event is caused by my present positive or negative thought about that event. If my thought about any past event is positive, my resulting feeling is positive. If my thought about any past event is negative, my resulting feeling is negative. If my thought of any past event is neutral, my feeling is neutral. It is part of human nature that I cannot always Alter a highly disturbing negative thought about a past event to some highly positive thought. But, at the minimum, I can Alter a highly disturbing negative thought to become a neutral thought. By doing that, I take back control of my life. I annihilate the sting of the negative memory of any past event. I accept the truth that regardless of my past, *I alone am responsible for how I feel every conscious moment of my life.* That is because my thought dwelling causes my feelings. By using SOAP I control my thought dwelling, therefore, I control my feelings.

GOOD LIFE TRUTHS
DERIVED FROM CHAPTER SEVEN

7-1.   Past events have no feelings in and of themselves.

7-2.   What occurred in my past does not cause the feelings I have in the present moment.

7-3.   It is by dwelling upon Satan-I negative thoughts about a feelingless past event that causes me to feel upset, immobilized, or discontented in the present moment.

7-4.   By utilizing SOAP, I can wash away all Satan-I negative thoughts about a feelingless past event, which brings me to peace with that feelingless past event.

7-5.   I alone am responsible for letting thoughts of a nonexistent, immutable, feelingless past event destroy my present moment peace of mind. I alone am responsible if I am not free from my feelingless past!

PART FOUR

BLAME AND RESPONSIBILITY AND SATAN'S THREE FIRE-BREATHING DRAGONS

CHAPTER EIGHT

BLAME AND RESPONSIBILITY

Satan-I, our constant nemesis, wants us to be at war with our respective pasts. That is because Satan-I thrives on troubled minds. To keep each of us troubled, Satan-I assumes the form of three distinct fire-breathing dragons. Each fire-breathing dragon is hell bent on destroying your enduring peace of mind. These fire-breathing dragons are:

1. The Other People Dragon: Remembering the horrible thing another person did to you in your past.
2. The Me Dragon: Dwelling on the thoughts of that really stupid thing you did, for which you cannot forgive yourself.
3. The Fate Dragon: Thinking about the terrible thing Fate did to you.

I want you to carefully note that there are only *three* types of things from your past that can deprive you of present moment peace of mind. Anything that is bothering you from your past *must* fall into one of these three categories. There are absolutely no exceptions. In terms of *negative thinking,* these three categories are:

1. Negative thought dwelling about that despicable thing another person did to you—The Other People Dragon.
2. Negative thought dwelling about that really stupid thing you did for which you cannot forgive yourself—The Me Dragon.
3. Negative thought dwelling about the horrible thing Fate did to you—The Fate Dragon.

You say, "I understand that Satan-I takes on the form of one or more of those three fire-breathing dragons to utterly destroy my enduring peace of mind. But how can I, a puny mortal, face and hope to vanquish any of those fire-breathing dragons?"

If left to your own powers, you can't; it would be utterly hopeless. However, by buckling on the armor of God you become invincible and are able to render impotent Satan's three dragons. Of course, this armor is utilizing the Good Life Truths, accepting your past as it really is, controlling your thought dwelling with the Stop, Obliterate, Alter, Praise methodology, utilizing the Healing Steps, which are given to you in later chapters, and never forgetting that *I can do all things through Him who gives me strength*! Thus armored, and drawing upon the strength of God Who exists at the center of your being, you are able to victoriously confront and slay any or all of Satan's three fire-breathing dragons that are feverishly attempting to destroy your enduring peace of mind.

The Two Kinds of Blame

Before marching off to confront Satan's first fire-breathing dragon, let us consider the concepts of blame and responsibility.

There are two very different classes of blame, societal blame and subjective blame. At all costs, we must keep those two classes of blame separated in our thinking. If we do not distinguish between the two types of blame, we will never be able to possess enduring peace of mind.

Societal blame is necessary to preserve the societal structure as we know and desire it. Societal blame deals with the types of wrongs to which all rational people in the society object. Societal blame subdivides into criminal guilt and civil liability. If a person commits a crime, he must be held blameworthy for committing that crime and should be punished accordingly. If a person commits a civil wrong, for example a personal injury, she should be held culpable and accountable for any damage she has caused. Societal blame is both necessary and good.

Then there is subjective blame. Subjective blame exists when you and I feel unhappy and we *blame* someone else or something for our feelings of unhappiness. We must find an object to *blame* for our feeling of unhappiness. You might *blame* your feeling of unhappiness on your spouse, children, doctor, lawyer, judge, the weather, floods, the stock market, etc. Subjective blame is one of Satan-I's most powerful weapons. Of course, the truth of the matter is that if you feel unhappy, someone else or something else is *never* to blame for your feeling of unhappiness. If you feel unhappy, without exception, *you* are to blame for your feeling of unhappiness. Your feeling of unhappiness is due to *your* erroneous Satan-I thinking. *Subjective blame is always wrong.*

Let me drive home with a poignant example the distinction between societal blame and subjective blame. Assume a despicable reprobate cruelly murdered my wife, my four children, my two daughters-in-law, my son-in-law, and my grandchildren, all of whom I love very much. I would want that person executed as punishment for the heinous murders he committed and as a deterrent to others who have the proclivity to commit like offenses. However, after a short grieving period, if I am to possess enduring peace of mind, I know I cannot *blame* that person for how I feel in the present moment! I hold that person socially blameful, but I would not hold him subjectively blameful for my present moment feelings. That villain does not cause my feelings. The thoughts I dwell upon cause my feelings. I would not give control of my life to that misfit. To the contrary, after a reasonable grieving period, I would begin praying for that poor lost soul.

But, I do not have to use a hypothetical anecdote to demonstrate this distinction. There is a perfect and real life example of the manner in which we should seperate societal blame and subjective blame. I gladly use as our standard bearer the actions of the Magnificent Pope John Paul II. When his would-be-assassin shot the Pontiff, clearly attempting to murder him, how did this venerable giant react? By going to the wretched man's prison cell, kneeling before him, *humbly* embracing him, and *lovingly* praying with him! However, the Holy Father never urged that the depraved soul be released from the criminal justice system nor spared the consequences of secular law. That is societal blame, and it must be dealt with for the well-being of us all. But, did the Pope hold one speck of personal hatred, anger, or ill feelings against that enemy of society? Actions speak much louder than words. That is being totally free of subjective blame.

Pope John Paul II followed the Christian concept of hating the sin, but loving the sinner. Do we follow that concept when someone wrongs us? That is our model and our goal.

Unfortunately many of us, like Perturbed Pamela, our disgruntled divorcee from Chapter Two, believe there is someone or something to *blame* when we feel bad, angry, unhappy, or despondent about something that occurred in our respective pasts. As lovingly as possible, I must tell you that if you believe that, you are sorely mistaken. Nothing could be further from the truth. Instead of accepting total and personal responsibility for your preset moment ill feelings, you are using *blame* to explain your feeling of unhappiness. You are using subjective *blame* by blaming someone else or something else for how you feel in the present moment. That type of thinking is wrong and must be corrected, or you will never enjoy enduring peace of mind.

As our wise and friendly divorcee, Luminary Mary, would tell us, "No other person or event is ever to blame for our ill feelings in the present moment." Past events cannot cause gnawing feelings of disquietude, unless we allow it. It is Satan-I stinking-thinking that causes us to feel unhappy. We must learn to take total responsibility for our ill feelings and learn how to overcome them.

Note well the point that is being made. Blaming someone else or something else for your ill feelings is antipodal to accepting total personal responsibility for how you feel in the present moment. These two concepts are mutually exclusive. You either *blame* someone else or something else for your ill feelings or you accept total personal responsibility for how you feel in the present moment. As always, it is entirely your choice. Do you choose to be like Luminary Mary, accepting responsibility for your feelings, or to be like Perturbed Pamela, blaming someone else for your present moment negative feelings? Do you choose God-I thinking or Satan-I stinking-thinking?

Sam Huddleston

Let me introduce you to Sam Huddleston, someone who made the transition from Satan-I stinking-thinking of blaming others for his discontentment to God-I positive thinking of accepting responsibility for his thoughts and actions. Unfortunately for Sam, he took a long and arduous road to make that transition.

Sam was born in a small town in Merced County. He was born to good stock. His father was a Sunday school superintendent. His grandfather was a deputy sheriff.

Sam's parents divorced when he was eight years old, a traumatic event for Sam. He was raised by his strong, God-fearing, God-loving father. Although poor, his father would accept no public assistance. His motto was, "Never let anyone do for you what you can do for yourself."

As happens to many people, Sam chose the wrong peer group. By the time he was thirteen years old, he was regularly drinking sloe gin. This progressed to the regular consumption of marijuana, uppers, downers, and even LSD. He went from stealing for excitement to stealing as a necessity to support his drinking and drug habits.

He was soon in the Merced County Juvenile Hall for a number of minor offenses. In due time his crimes escalated to forgery, burglary, and assault with a deadly weapon. He carried a knife with him as his constant companion. (Big mistake!)

Of course, there was plenty of sex. By the time he was sixteen years old he had fathered a son.

Then there was a week of nonstop alcohol, drugs, and girls. At the end of this infamous week, the revelers had no money, no drugs, nor any alcohol to drink. In a drunken stupor, Sam and his two cousins decided to rob a liquor store.

One cousin stayed as get-away driver while Sam and the other cousin proceeded into the store. Sam gave his trusty knife to his cousin, for what he thought was going to be a robbery. Instead, his cousin stabbed to death the liquor store manager. That made Sam an accomplice to murder.

Not surprisingly, the trio was immediately apprehended. Although only seventeen years of age, the Merced County Superior Court Judge ruled that Sam should be tried as an adult. Before trial, Sam's attorney negotiated a plea bargain with the District Attorney for second degree murder. Sam accepted the plea bargain.

Sam was incarcerated in a California prison for almost five years. Fortunately, in prison he returned to the faith of his fathers. He came to know and accept Jesus as his personal Lord and Savior. By doing that, he made the change from subjectively *blaming* other people for his feelings and finally accepting total responsibility for his thought dwelling and resulting feelings.

I met Sam many years ago. He made a lasting impression on me. I highly recommend his book, *Five Years To Life*. (At that time in California, second degree murder carried a term of five years to life; thus the title of Sam's book. It is now fifteen years to life.)

Without any editing on my part, here is what Sam has to say about learning to take personal responsibility for our thought dwelling and feelings, rather than looking for something or someone else to *blame* for our feelings. This scene took place while Sam was in the California Department of Corrections:

> My telephone time was up; the next dude was waiting. I walked out into the yard feeling lonelier than I ever had in my life. I thought about something Daddy used to say. If we ever came to a point in life when we needed a friend and no one was there, God would always be at our side, waiting. "Closer than hands and feet," Daddy used to say.

I flopped down on the grass and looked up at the stars. Where was God? Someone else who was supposed to be there, and wasn't. "I can see my hands and feet," I said out loud, "but I sure can't see You."

I waited a moment, half-hopeful, but I saw nothing, heard nothing. Except my own voice—my voice as I'd never heard it before. *It's their fault.* They made me drink. It's George's fault. He snitched on Shep and me. It's Mama's fault. She went away. It's Daddy's fault. It's God's fault.

And then a voice that was definitely not my own: "*Sam, how long are you going to blame others for the choices you make?*"

The grass was damp, the wet soaking through my clothes, but I sat there stunned, listening to thoughts in my head that I knew weren't my thoughts. "When are you going to take charge of your life, Sam? I can't help you with your life until it's yours. Not David's. Not your mother's. When are you going to take control of your life?"

"God," I whispered hoarsely, "is this You?" Knowing it was. Knowing these ideas weren't coming from me. "God, if You're really there . . . really here . . . if it's all true, like Daddy says, . . . God, I'm not asking to go home. I'm just asking You to help me change. Now. Here in prison. It's right—what You said—I'm in prison because I fouled up. Me. No one else. Over and over. But God, if You're real, and if You'll help me, I'm going to be different."

In a conversation with a fellow prisoner, Huddleston relates another experience:

Other Prisoner (OP): "What happened? How come you wanted to be a Christian?"

Sam (S): "*Man, all my life I've been blaming other people for my problems.* I blamed God, white folks, my parents, everyone I knew. Except me. I felt empty inside. And things just got worse and I couldn't sleep at night."

OP: "Me neither."

S: "So finally one night I was by myself here in the yard."

OP: "Here at Sierra?"

S: "Right here where we're standing. And it was like God said, *Hey, man, when are you going to take responsibility for your own life?*"

OP: "God really said that? I mean, is God real?"

S: "Listen, all I know is I have this kind of smile inside that I never had before and which I don't understand how it got there."

OP: "Hey, can I become a Christian?"

S: "Sure."

OP: "When?"

S: "I guess now. Just tell God it's your own fault you messed up, ask Him to help you change." He prayed and as he did he cried. I didn't know what to do; I cried with him.

Do not miss the important transition Sam made from subjectively blaming other people for his feelings to accepting total, personal responsibility for his thought dwelling and feelings. Sam made the successful transition from a Perturbed Pamela disposition to a Luminary Mary disposition. When it comes to finally taking personal responsibility for our thoughts and feelings, Sam is the model to follow.

After prison, Sam graduated from Bethany College, attended Golden Gate Baptist Theological Seminary, obtained his master's degree in counseling through Azusa Pacific University, and became President of the Match-Two Prisoner Outreach Program, the largest one-to-one prisoner visitation program in the nation.

Sam concludes his book with the following statement:

Often, as I look back over my life so far, I realize that my change started in a stinky prison. It was there I decided that *if my life was to change, I would have to take responsibility for it. I could no longer blame others.* It was then, by the help of almighty God, that I realized no situation is permanent. Change can and will happen—for me and for you, too—if we let God in. (All emphasis added.)

If you are *blaming* anyone or anything that happened in your past for your present moment unhappiness, you are absolutely wrong. You are absolutely correct when you *blame* your Satan-I thought dwelling for your unhappiness. But fear not. As Sam Huddleston did, so you can overhaul your manner of thinking. You can fearlessly face and slay Satan's three fire-breathing dragons. You can make everlasting peace with your past.

If you are not yet doing it, you will soon be saying and meaning: *I alone am responsible for how I feel every conscious moment of my life.*

You must take full responsibility for assembling and completing your own personal good life puzzle. You must take full responsibility for drawing upon the God-I Force within you to drive away from underneath your own personal cherry tree. If you do, life becomes a very exciting journey. If you don't: *Plop. Plop. Plop.*

Synopsis

Say to yourself:

Except for God, I am the only person totally committed to and responsible for my enduring peace of mind. I can arrive at a state of enduring peace of mind by relentlessly taking control of my thought dwelling. An extremely important part of controlling my thought dwelling is to forever eliminate subjective blame from my thinking. Every time I have thoughts of blaming someone or something for my present moment unhappiness, I must immediately and without exception SOAP away such thoughts. Subjective blame must once and for all be eradicated from my thinking process. I will kill, kill, kill all Satan-I thoughts of blaming someone or something for any ill feelings I have in the present moment. I have reached blame maturity when I can truthfully say, "I alone am responsible for how I feel every conscious moment of my life."

GOOD LIFE TRUTHS
DERIVED FROM CHAPTER EIGHT

8-1.   Societal blame is good. It is indispensable for maintaining an orderly society that guarantees its members life, liberty, and the pursuit of happiness.

8-2.   Subjective blame is vile. It is one of the greatest weapons Satan-I uses to destroy my enduring peace of mind. If Satan-I can lead me into a subjective blame state of mind, he owns me.

8-3.   Nothing from my past is to blame for my feeling of being unhappy in the present moment. If I feel unhappy in the present moment, I alone am to blame for my feeling of unhappiness. My feeling of unhappiness is due to my erroneous Satan-I subjective blame stinking-thinking.

8-4.   At all costs, I must forever eradicate subjective blame from my thinking process. I will never again blame anyone or anything for how I feel in the present moment.

8-5.   By controlling my thought dwelling, I prevent Satan-I thoughts of subjective blame from ever causing me unhappiness in the present moment. That will bring me to enduring peace of mind. That will raise me to a higher level of consciousness.

CHAPTER NINE

What Another Person Did to You in Your Past Does Not Determine How You Feel in the Present Moment

As we discussed earlier, anything from our individual pasts that bothers us *must* fall into one of three categories, there are *absolutely* no exceptions. The three categories are thinking negatively about:

1. What another person did to me: The Other People Dragon.
2. That really stupid thing I did: The Me Dragon
3. What Fate did to me: The Fate Dragon.

By understanding that fact alone, you are able to methodically divide, overpower, and slay Satan's three dreadful dragons. And once you slay Satan's accursed dragons, you shall have made final and everlasting peace with your past.

And how, my dear reader, shall we be equipped to face these villainous creatures who destroy peace of mind? Together, we buckle onto our left arms the invicible shields of knowing our pasts are unchangeable, feelingless, and nonexistent (except in our memories). In our right hands we fearlessly wield the mighty sword of Stop, Obliterate, Alter, Praise. And for almost infinite strength, we recognize and draw upon God, Who resides at the center of our beings. Together, we triumphantly shout, *"I can do all things through Him who stregthens me!"*

Thus equipped, we fearlessly confront and do battle with Satan-I in the form of the first fire-breathing, peace of mind destroying dragon, the Other People Dragon.

You rightly say to me, "Donned with the armor you have given me, I do not hesitate to engage in combat with Satan-I in the form of the Other People Dragon. But, since I am battling a mental and not a physical demon, how will I know when I have slain this beast that I cannot see?" A good question.

I reply, "You will know you have slain the Other People Dragon when you no longer experience burning stings when you think about those abhorrent things another person did to you. When your thoughts of those transgressions are only thoughts of an historical event and not emotionally disturbing thoughts, then you have slain the Other People Dragon. He lies dead at your feet. You are at peace."

You say, "Let us begin the conquest. I am eager to experience unceasing peace of mind!"

Accepting Responsibility for Our Thought Dwelling

To slay the Other People Dragon we mightily strike the first blow by taking complete responsibility for our thought dwelling.

Let us return to the stories of our two divorcees, Luminary Mary and Perturbed Pamela. Keep in mind that Mary teaches us how to slay the Other People Dragon. Pamela teaches us how to be consumed by the Other People Dragon.

If you recall, Mary received virtually nothing from her divorce, except the obligation to raise four children on her own. Mary is not formally educated. However, she is very wise. Although she may have never articulated, I *alone am responsible for how I feel every conscious moment of my life*, she is a living model of that Good Life Truth.

Because of the manner in which her former husband treated Mary, much injustice came into her life. But, she never *thinks* in terms of injustice or unhappiness. Furthermore, she never *thinks* in terms of *blaming* her former husband for how she feels in the present moment. Therefore, she experiences no feeling of discontentment in the present moment. Mary takes full responsibility for her thought dwelling and the feelings that result therefrom. She habitually practices Stop, Obliterate, Alter, Praise to control her thought dwelling.

Mary *chooses* to be thankful for all she possesses. The thoughts she chooses to dwell upon are about her beautiful children and grandchildren and how very dearly they love her. Her Satan-I is a big loser. She has given her mind over to God-I. She is one of life's winners. Her good-life puzzle is very complete.

In contrast, we recall Perturbed Pamela who received a beautiful home, luxury automobile, and millions of dollars as a result of her divorce. Nothing anyone says to Pamela can dissuade her from hating her former husband. She constantly dwells upon many evil thoughts about him. Since she *thinks* negatively about him, she *feels* negatively about him. She *blames* him for how she feels in the present moment. Her bad feelings constantly gnaw on her. She is a living model of enduring discontentment. Even though she is well educated and has a relatively high IQ, she is totally unaware of the fact that she can control her thought dwelling. Instead of controlling her thought dwelling, she *allows* herself to unremittingly dwell upon her Satan-I thoughts about her former husband and their divorce. She *allows* her Satan-I to blind her of all the tangible and intangible things she possesses. Satan-I *owns* her mind. As a result, she indulges in self-pity and seeks pity from others. Her Satan-I is having a heyday.

We can learn much from Pamela who does not SOAP away her Satan-I negative thoughts about her divorce. By choosing to dwell upon negative *thoughts* about her divorce, it is inescapable that Pamela cannot move beyond negative *feelings* about her divorce. As she sees it, her ex-husband and the way he treated her cause her bad feelings. *He* is to blame for her ill-feelings. She couldn't be more mistaken. Pamela will not recognize a most important Good Life Truth:

> It is not at all important what another person did to me in my past. It is most important what thoughts I dwell upon relating to what that person did to me in my past.

Pamela is rigidly parked under her cherry tree, foot firmly fixed on the brake pedal of her mind. To her, life stinks. *Plop. Plop. Plop.*

Stop, Obliterate, Alter, Praise never occurs to Pamela. She has no idea that she alone is responsible for controlling the thoughts she dwells upon, and therefore, responsible for her feelings. Her good life puzzle is in a state of chaos.

If Pamela were to practice Stop, Obliterate, Alter, Praise, she could enjoy a four-fold benefit:

1. By choosing not to dwell on her Satan-I negative thoughts about her divorce, she rids herself of bad feelings about her divorce. If she Obliterates the negative thoughts about her former husband, she Obliterates her negative feelings about him.

2. Pamela would no longer have to *blame* her former husband for her bad feelings. The fewer hate objects we have in life, the better we feel about ourselves and about life. When you hear someone say, "It's all his fault," you know that person does not understand the relationship of subjective blaming, self-responsibility, controlling one's thought dwelling, and present moment feelings. The practice of *not* subjectively blaming other people for our bad feelings automatically forces us to take full responsibility

for our own feelings. Not having to blame someone for how we feel is really exciting!

3. Pamela could be enjoying the present precious moment with family and friends, with warm thoughts about her children, grandchildren, all she possesses, or with happy expectations about the future. Instead, she wastes this precious present moment with Satan-I negative thoughts about her former husband.

4. Pamela would like herself better. Also, many of her friends would like her better.

What a terrible thing it is to waste the present moment on Satan-I negative thought dwelling about our nonexistent, immutable, feelingless past! Again, I borrow a Good Life Truth from Chapter One, a truth by which Mary lives:

> I must never let what happened in one of my yesterdays destroy the peace of my today.

Here we have two divorces handled by the same attorney, in the same courthouse, with the same judge, at approximately the same time, with diametrically opposed resulting feelings.

Mary chooses to dwell upon her God-I positive thoughts about her children, grandchildren, and how much they love her as her way of life, leading to her enduring peace of mind. She is content with what little she has. Pamela chooses to dwell only upon her Satan-I negative thoughts of how she perceives her husband treated her as her way of life, leading to enduring discontentment. She is never content, despite all she possesses.

The stories of Luminary Mary and Perturbed Pamela provide very strong evidence that it is not what another person did to us that causes us to feel present moment contentment or discontentment. The type of thoughts we choose to dwell upon about past events cause us to feel contentment or discontentment in the present moment.

If we are wise, we will only dwell upon God-I positive thoughts about what another person did to us in our pasts. We learn how to do that when we get to the upcoming Healing Steps. This will lead to our feeling content and positive. It will lead to God's peace in our hearts.

If we are not wise, we get stuck in negative thought dwelling about what other people did to us in our pasts. Then we get stuck under our respective cherry trees. *Plop. Plop. Plop.*

I pray that by now you are absolutely convinced that there is a cause and effect relationship between the thoughts you dwell upon and how you feel in the present moment. And since you have the power to control your thought dwelling, you alone are responsible for your contentment or discontentment.

Consider two other cases that corroborate that realization:

Inconsolable Ivan

When Ivan was six years old, his uncle forced Ivan to touch the uncle's penis through the uncle's pants. That happened on three separate occasions. Ivan is now forty-eight years old. Although he was in counseling for more than twenty years, he never recovered from those incidents of sexual abuse that occurred more than forty years ago.

I am in regular contact with Ivan. At his insistence, we often discuss his long past sexual abuse. I try to convince him that Satan-I, in the form of the Other People Dragon, wants him to dwell upon thoughts of the past evil his uncle perpetrated and that God-I wants him to put the memory of the event behind him and get on with his life. But to no avail, the Other People Dragon has consumed Ivan.

Ivan is like a broken record, "You have no idea what it's like. Even though he's dead, I can't forgive him for what he did to me. I hate him so much!"

Ivan openly admits that he dwells upon these negative thoughts and that he experiences the resulting negative feelings. But, in his words, "I can't help it. You just don't know what it's like! These things he did to me affect my relationships with other people. Even when I'm having intercourse with my wife, I think about it. I hate him so much!"

As with Perturbed Pamela, it is never a satisfying experience being in Ivan's company. To his close friends he avows he seldom talks about his sexual abuse. Such is not the case. It seems to us his abuse is all he wants to talk about. His negativity is overwhelming. Ivan is rigidly parked under his cherry tree. Satan-I owns his mind. *Plop. Plop. Plop.*

Wise David

When David was six years of age, a neighbor boy viciously sodomized him. That occurred on four different occasions. David tells me he knew those acts were vile. However, he was wise enough to realize he was not at all culpable for the sodomy.

David told me his story when we were discussing my writing this book. He never before related that experience to anyone.

David is now in his mid-fifties. He warrants that at no time in his life did he experience a crisis over the sodomy.

I smiled broadly when he told me that whenever a thought of the sexual abuse came into his mind, he elected to dismiss it in favor of a more pleasant thought. In his words, "That happened a long time ago. It's over. It's done. To me, it's ancient history. Further, I know I can never change what was done to me. Why should I keep thinking about something that can never be changed?

"I've also been able to keep things in proper perspective. I assure you, Mike, the sodomy was disgusting and revolting. But, many of my relatives were in Russia during World War II. Some of them were executed. Some of them starved to death. Would I change places with any of them? Not for all the money in the world.

"I'm certain that being raised in a good Christian home also helped. My mother was an incredible woman. Although we were lower middle-class, we were taught never to think about anything bad or what we didn't have. Instead, we were taught to think only about good things and to thank God for all that we possessed.

"Do you know what my mother thanked God for, over and over again? A thermostat! I'm not kidding, a thermostat. She grew up in the days of hauling wood and coal for the stove and furnace. Then someone had to remove and dispose of ashes in the bitter cold Ohio winters. It was her job to help with those chores. She sure loved her thermostat. By the push of a lever she could have heating or cooling. Never more did she have to contend with wood, coal, or ashes. I wonder how many people in our day and age thank God for their thermostats?

"That was contagious. Ever since I can remember, I've been thanking God for all I possess. Yes, I especially thank Him for my *two* thermostats. I never dreamed I would own a house so big that it required *two* furnaces and *two* thermostats! The more I thank Him, and the more I share, the more I get. It's unbelievable!"

David continued, "Why would I ever dwell upon thoughts of those ancient events that occurred over fifty years ago and allow it to diminish the quality of my life? Why would anyone?

"My mother was correct. I choose not to think about the bad things that occurred in my life. I choose to thank God for all the wonderful things I possess. Why would I do otherwise? Why would anyone do that?

"I assure you that at the present time, thoughts of the sodomy are virtually nonexistent. On those rare occasions when a thought of those events enters my mind, it has no emotional impact on me. I summarily dismiss such thoughts."

When I discussed the Stop, Obliterate, Alter, Praise methodology with David, he broke into laughter, "Boy, that's great! I certainly never thought about it in those terms, but I believe that's what I've been doing all my life. Thank you for giving me a label for my thinking process. I like SOAP."

David is happy, wealthy, popular, and a success by any standard. He gives unselfishly of his time and his resources to his church and the community at large, especially to those in financial and emotional need. It is a superb pleasure being in his company. He has given his mind to God-I. God has rewarded him richly for *choosing* to do that.

We have two individuals who were sexually molested at the same age. After more than forty years, Ivan is still unable to deal with his sexual abuse. He has a miserable life. At a very young age, David promptly and with finality dealt with his sexual abuse. His life is very good.

Why are those two victims, both sexually abused at approximately the same age, so different in their present day feelings? What makes the less sexually abused Ivan so negative and the viciously sodomized David so positive?

We know the answers to those questions.

Inconsolable Ivan continually dwells upon Satan-I negative thoughts about the sexual abuse at the hands of his uncle. He is ignorant of the fact that he has the God-I Power within him right now to Obliterate those thoughts from his mind whenever they occur. Once his Satan-I negative thoughts are Obliterated, his corresponding negative feelings will cease to exist. By dwelling upon Satan-I negative thoughts of his sexual abuse, he *chooses* to sit under the cherry tree with his foot firmly pressed against the brake pedal of his mind. *Plop. Plop. Plop.*

On the other hand, by taking control of his thought dwelling, Wise David seldom thinks about his sodomy. To him, it is over and done, not to be thought about. It is historical, not emotional. He is truly wise. His good-life puzzle is complete. He is very close to his God-I. He would never stop under our proverbial cherry tree.

Obviously, it is not what anyone did to you in your past that determines your contentment or discontentment in the present moment. It is the type of thoughts which you *choose* to dwell upon that determines how you feel in the present moment.

An especially tailored Good Life Truth naturally follows from this discussion:

> I alone am responsible for how I feel every conscious moment of my life, regardless of the injustices other people perpetrated upon me in my past.

There is almost infinite evidence that proposition is true. Often in the extreme cases that truth becomes self-evident. Therefore, let us consider the famous Austrian psychiatrist, Victor Frankl.

Victor Frankl

During World War II, Frankl was sent to Auschwitz, Dachau, and other concentration camps. His father, mother, brother, and wife died in concentration camps.

Frankl was systematically stripped of all his possessions, including each hair that was shaved from his body. He suffered or witnessed virtually every indignity man could inflict upon his fellow man. He was treated in a manner none of us would dream about in our worst nightmare. Yet, he never lost hope, always maintaining a positive attitude.

How was he able to do that? As Professor Gordon Allport states in the introduction to Frankl's book, *Man's Search for Meaning:*

> "Hunger, humiliation, fear and deep anger at injustice are rendered tolerable by closely guarded *images* (God-I positive thoughts) of beloved persons, by religion, by a grim sense of humor, and even by glimpses of the healing beauties of nature—a tree or a sunset."

How many other prisoners unceasingly cursed their guards? How many were consumed with hate and detestation for their captors? What did Frankl *choose* to think about? Images of beloved persons, religion, and glimpses of the healing beauties of nature—a tree or a sunset. What did less wise captives think about? Hate, hate, and more hate.

Compare those last mentioned individuals with Christian saints who were marched into the Roman Coliseum to be devoured by wild animals. They had peace in their hearts, prayed for their captors, and with great expectation and excitement, looked forward to being united with their God.

And how about Jesus? Regardless of your religious convictions, He was an innocent man nailed to a cross, who died an ignominious death. Some of His last words were, "Forgive them Father, for they know not what they do." Who had the greater peace of mind, Jesus the victim or the killer high-priests whose hearts were filled with rage, anger, and hate for this innocent man?

And how about you? Although you have undergone painful trauma at the hands of another person, with your whole heart you must come to believe that unless *you* allow it, what happened to you in your past does not control how you feel in the present moment. This includes being physically abused, sexually abused, tortured in a concentration camp, losing a child through the fault of another person, maimed, lied about, or suffering any other inequity at the hands of another person.

It is by your thought dwelling that you determine your feelings and outlook on life every conscious moment of your life. No matter what anyone did to you in your past, if you are wise, you choose not to dwell upon Satan-I negative thoughts about that person or the event. You choose not to let your nonexistent, immutable, feelingless past affect how you feel in the present moment. You SOAP those thoughts out of your mind. You choose to dwell upon thoughts that raise your self-esteem. You are a good person. You deserve the good life. Your puzzle should be complete. God wants it to be complete.

Feeling Powerless

Some people believe that what another person did to them somehow mysteriously takes away their power to have enduring peace of mind. Nothing could be further from the truth.

There is no question that some people *do* let what another person did to them take away their enduring peace of mind. But that is a *choice* they make by *choosing* not to control their thought dwelling.

If it was unconditionally and universally binding that one human being could divest another human being of the feelings of peace and contentment, there never would be a Luminary Mary, a Wise David, an Adeline Hider, or a Victor Frankl. But, the world abounds with these types of people. As we say in the legal community, *Res Ipsa Loquitur,* the thing speaks for itself.

It is unequivocally clear that, unless *you* allow it, no person can take away your power to possess enduring peace of mind. When we allow the memory of what someone did to us to destroy our present moment contentment, we do give control of our lives to that person. We must *never* allow that to happen.

Your Satan-I desires that you believe that perpetrator has divested you of your power to be content because your Satan-I cannot feed on content minds. By the degree to which you fail to practice Stop, Obliterate, Alter, Praise, you alone choose how much control of your life you give over to your Satan-I, taking on the form of the Other People Dragon. Depending on how much time you give to dwelling on Satan-I negative thoughts about what that person did to you, you give no control, some control, or total control of your mind to your Satan-I. You are rendered powerless only if you *think* you are powerless. Dwelling on the thought of being powerless makes you feel powerless.

Again I remind you, there is a tremendous difference between what another person did to you and your now having bad feelings about what another person did to you. We cannot avoid bad experiences. However, we can avoid bad feelings, regardless of bad experiences.

What was done to you in your past, was done to you in your past. It's over. It's forever done. It's ancient history. It can never be changed.

How you feel in the present moment, is how you feel in the present moment. Your feelings are now. Your feelings can only exist in the present. Unlike unchangeable past events, feelings can be readily changed. That is the only thing that makes spiritual mending possible. A most loving God wants to help us. All we have to do is to allow Him to help us.

Talk to yourself. It's alright. I do it all the time. Listen to yourself. Take responsibility for your thought dwelling. If you do, ultimately you will come to realize:

1. Thinking negatively about what that other person did to me causes me to feel negative in the present moment.
2. I alone control how long I dwell upon any negative thought which enters my mind.

3. Therefore, I alone am responsible if I feel negative about what that other person did to me in my past.

If someone hurt you in your past, whether it be your spouse, child, best friend, relative, neighbor, fellow-employee, or total stranger, do you choose to be a Luminary Mary, Perturbed Pamela, Inconsolable Ivan, Wise David, or Victor Frankl? Are you wise or unaware? You alone choose how you feel every conscious moment of your life. *No one, but no one, can make you feel any way you choose not to feel.* You are absolutely free to determine how you feel in the present moment. All you have to do is make the right choices about your thought dwelling.

It is only by accepting this awesome responsibility for your thought dwelling, which causes your feelings, that you can achieve enduring peace of mind. Only by accepting that responsibility can your puzzle be complete. You must never again think or speak of *blaming* another person for how you feel in the present moment. Subjective blame must be expunged from your vocabulary.

I *alone* am responsible for how I feel every conscious moment of my life.

The only person who can prevent you from overcoming Satan-I self-defeating, negative thoughts of past trauma is you. Unless you allow it, it is impossible for another person to make you feel hateful, envious, jealous, inferior, depressed, mad, angry, disgusted, or powerless. As difficult as that may be for you to accept, and I say this as lovingly as possible, you alone choose to be stopped under your cherry tree.

If you are stopped under your cherry tree, lift your foot from the brake pedal. Let's zoom away. A beautiful world awaits us.

Being Realistic

What is it that Luminary Mary, Wise David, my mother, Victor Frankl, and millions of content people intuitively understand about overcoming and healing deep mental wounds inflicted by another person? How did they go about slaying the Other People Dragon?

Let us consider two facts that lay the foundation for the Healing Steps.

Fact One: There are many people over whom you have no control who will bring trauma into you life.

We discussed divorces, sexual abuse, and concentration camps. We could endlessly add to that list: drunk drivers, murderers, rapists, thieves, gang members, and out of control teenagers who daily bring grief into countless lives. As a judge, I deal with the victims of those people on a daily basis. I assure you the victims are as diverse in their outlooks and feelings about their trauma as are Mary, Pamela, Ivan, David, Frankl, and everyone else we've met to this point.

Each of us can easily name a number of people who unjustifiably and grievously offended us in life's journey. Life is far from perfect. If we naively expect to go through life without people hurting us, we are destined for serious problems. We are not being realistic. It has never happened to anyone. It never will happen to anyone. We are no exceptions. Jesus said:

> In this world you *will* have trouble. But take heart! I have overcome the world. (John 16:33 NIV)

Notice, Jesus did not say "if you have trouble," but, you "*will*" have trouble.

And from the Old Testament we learn:

> When you pass through the waters, I will be with you; and when you pass through the rivers, they will not sweep over you. When you walk through the fire, you will not be burned; the flames will not set you ablaze. (Isa. 43:2 NIV)

As my dear friend Pastor Bill Stephens says of that passage, "It is never a question of 'will I pass through deep waters,' it is a statement. Somewhere in your life you *will* suffer persecution, tribulation, go through deep water, sometimes to the point of almost being overwhelmed. The lesson here is that no matter the cause of your trouble, the Lord will never forsake you."

It is unrealistic and foolish to expect to go through life without people hurting you. Accepting that fact, it is wise to know how to deal with the injustices people bring into your life.

Fact Two: We only have bad feelings towards people about whom we have negative thoughts.

If you intensely hate a person, you may have to begin by punching a pillow, screaming aloud, or seeking professional help. However, ultimately you're going to have to fix yourself. But, how do we do that? How can we ever forgive someone for divorcing us, for sexually molesting us, or for placing and torturing us in a concentration camp?

Hate and Healing

Wise people know the following three truths about hate and healing:

Truth One: When I hate another person, I do not hurt the person I hate. The only person I hurt is myself.

Your hate is your hate. You own it. It is your private possession. Only you can dispose of it.

Truth Two: It is impossible for me to have enduring peace of mind so long as I hate one other human being.

And what are you choosing to do to yourself if you harbor hate for another human being? You give control of your life to your Satan-I and he loves it. Because you hate another person, stomach acids are churning. You prepare fertile ground for an ulcer. Your blood pressure is elevated. You think hate, hate, hate, morning, noon, and night. Stress is building. There is more fertile ground for psychosomatic problems. Yes sir, you're really fixing that other person by hating him so much! It should be obvious that the only person you are hurting is yourself.

It should also be obvious that so long as you harbor such feelings against another person, you will never possess that greatest of all treasures: the feeling of inner peace, God's contentment, and enduring peace of mind. Forgive your transgressor for a very selfish reason. Forgive him or her because you want to possess enduring peace of mind.

You say, "But you don't understand, just look at what that person did to me!"

And I tell you, I understand the feelings of being powerless, worthless, the terrible trap of searching for pity from others, and indulging in self-pity. I understand Satan-I.

I've had good friends and relatives grievously hurt me. I wanted people to pity me. I indulged in self-pity. I didn't like it very much. In fact, I didn't like it at all. If you are of that state of mind, and are honest with yourself, you will admit you don't like it either.

Truth Three: I must forgive my transgressor because God has ordered me to do so.

> No matter the wrong, do no violence to your neighbor. (Hate is violence.) (Sirach 10:6 NAB)

We are all familiar with the famous admonition that unless we forgive those who hurt us, our heavenly Father will not find it in His heart to forgive us. Stop and think about that for a moment. That is really, really scary!

> For if you forgive men their trespasses, your heavenly Father will also forgive you. But if you do not forgive men their trespasses, *neither will your Father forgive your trespasses.* (Matt. 6:14–15 NKJV)

> And whenever you stand praying, if you have anything against anyone, forgive him, that your Father in heaven may also forgive you your trespasses. But if you do not forgive, *neither will your Father in heaven forgive your trespasses.* (Mark 11:25–26 NKJV)

God could not make His message clearer. If we don't forgive those who trespass against us, the consequences are truly terrifying! And, as the author of Proverbs wisely tells us:

> A man's wisdom gives him patience; it is to his glory to overlook an offense. (Prov. 19:11 NIV)

But, God has the audacity to even ask more of you than just forgiving your enemy, He wants you to love and pray for that dirtbag who hurt you so bad! Incredible!

Jesus says:

> You have heard that it was said, 'You shall love your neighbor and hate your enemy.' But I say to you, love your enemies and pray for those who persecute you. (Matthew 6:43:44 NAB)

Of course, God is no fool. He wants us to pray for our enemy so we can overcome our hate for that person, so that we can possess enduring peace of mind! God's plan is always the best plan!

Do you want to be healed of your hatred? Then, no matter how much it hurts, you must pray daily for your enemy. Even if you are an atheist, you must pray daily for your enemy. What do you have to lose? Praying to what you believe to be a nonexistent God can't hurt you, and it might even help you.

It may be difficult at first, but you must persevere. It doesn't have to be a long or eloquent prayer. Simply say, "Dear God, please give her enduring peace of mind." That's all, nothing more, nothing less. But you must pray it everyday until you mean it and your hate subsides. It works. And it works because God says it will work.

By praying that your enemy has enduring peace of mind, you accomplish two important things:

First, you eradicate the hate you feel against your enemy since you cannot be praying for her enduring peace of mind and hating her at the same time.

Second, if God grants your enemy enduring peace of mind, she cannot hate you. As we know, a person cannot have enduring peace of mind and simultaneously hate another human being. They are mutually exclusive. Therefore, there is that much less hate in the world, which is always good. And you benefit because there is one less person in the world who hates you. That is also good.

Praying for your enemy is a win-win situation. It is absolutely necessary for your well-being. It is an integral part of forgiving someone who seriously offended you. It makes negative memories of your feelingless past truly feelingless. These past events become only historical events and thinking about them no longer carries any emotional baggage. You begin to forgive, and thereby think less often of the person who raped you, the drunk driver who killed your loving spouse, or the concentration camp guards who led you to the brink of death.

You can truly say, "I forgive you. What you did to me is now only an historical event in my memory bank. There is no longer any anger or hate in my heart toward you. You no longer have any control over me. You no longer can hurt me. I wish both you and myself enduring peace of mind."

The transgression is no longer your problem. It may still be a problem for the transgressor, but it is no longer your problem. And isn't that what this is all about? You worked through your problem. That's all that is important to you. You regained your enduring peace of mind. You are a winner in the game of life. Your good-life puzzle is coming together. You pulled away from your cherry tree.

Mental health practitioners can provide valuable guidance, but it is only by your self-effort that you will be healed. You must accept the responsibility of transforming yourself from a negative state of mind to a positive state of mind. You do that by following the Healing Steps.

The Healing Steps to Completely Forgive Someone Who Has Hurt You

Now, we come to the Healing Steps you must follow if you truly desire to be healed of hatred because of what another person did to you.

I must warn you, this is the acid test. If you refuse to give your affirmation to any statement associated with a particular Healing Step, it is a certain indication Satan has a death grip on your mind. If you are unwilling to give that affirmation, you may not be ready to be healed from the memories of what another person did to you in your past. That could mean you still desire pity from other people or you want to continue to wallow in your own self-pity, "Oh, poor me!" Unfortunately, it may be that you find your self-worth in what that person did to you. If Satan does have such a death grip on your mind, he will do everything he can to keep you from being healed. At all costs you must fight Satan, one Healing Step at a time!

You go through the healing process by affirming each of the Healing Step statements. Dwell upon each thought for a few moments as you go through the healing process. It is important that you proceed through the Healing Steps in the order in which they are presented.

As you make your journey through the Healing Steps, there is one almost sacred rule you must not violate: Only when you can *truthfully affirm* any given statement, should you proceed to the next Healing Step. In other words, you must take one Step at a time. Do not proceed to the next Healing Step until you truly believe in your heart the truth of the statement in the Healing Step you are presently contemplating. Do not proceed until you can *truthfully* say, "Yes, I accept this truth. I agree with it. I will make it part of my way of thinking."

Repeat the process as often as necessary. Be assured this procedure will restore your enduring peace of mind, *if* you are *ready* to be healed.

With courage, God's love, and God's Power at the center of your being, let us proceed to confront and slay the Other People Dragon:

1. *I accept the fact that I am not singled out for trauma caused by other people.*

    I realize trauma caused by other people flows into the lives of everyone who ever lived. Trauma is part of the human experience. There are absolutely no exceptions. I am no exception. I am ready to no longer feel, Why me! Oh, poor me! I am ready to be healed.

2. *I must get my traumatic incident and recovery into proper perspective.*

I know what that person did to me wasn't good. In fact, it was very bad. However, it could have been a lot worse. I know there are people who were in concentration camps, brutally tortured, starved, physically mutilated, and gang raped, but they made peace with their pasts.

There is an important distinction here that I must not miss. I may not find comfort in the fact that other people suffered greater atrocities than I suffered. What I find in my comparison is *hope* in the fact that other people suffered greater atrocities than I suffered, and they made peace with their pasts.

As painful as it is for me to say this, what happened to me wasn't nearly as bad as what happened to many other people. They found enduring peace of mind. I know I can also put my trauma behind me and find enduring peace of mind. If they did it, I can do it, *if I want to!*

3. *Without God, I admit I am powerless against Satan in the form of the Other People Dragon.*

I admit I am powerless against Satan in the form of the Other People Dragon. It is only by drawing upon the greater Power of the Holy Spirit Who dwells within me that I am able to defeat the Other People Dragon. Once I submit I know that *I can do all things through Him Who gives me strength.* I then become invincible against my Satan-I. From this day forward, I solemnly promise to draw upon the Power of God within me to vanquish the Other People Dragon. I do this by acknowledging that the Holy Spirit is at the center of my being and humbly seeking His assistance.

4. *To be healed from the negative memories of what another person did to me means that I am willing to take full responsibility for how I feel in the present moment.*

I truly desire to be healed from the heinous memories of what that person did to me. I know healing carries with it awesome peace. However, I realize healing also carries with it awesome responsibility. I can no longer *blame* that person for how I feel in the present moment. I am willing to accept total responsibility for my present moment feelings. I will never again *blame* that person for how I feel in the present moment.

5. *What another person did to me is a dead event that can no longer hurt me.*

All that really exists is the present moment. That past transgression is completely dead. It died the moment it was over. That thing that happened to me is gone forever. The act can never again hurt me. It lives only in my memory. It is an event without substance. Only negatively thinking about that event can hurt me. If that nonexistent event cannot hurt me, but my thoughts about that event continue to hurt me, it is obvious that I must overhaul my thinking process. I choose to overhaul my thinking process starting right now.

6. *What another person did to me is a changeless event. I should not be disturbed by thoughts of a changeless event.*

The richest, the most powerful, the most brilliant people in the world cannot change one speck of their pasts, no matter how much they may desire to do so. Like them, nothing I do will change one speck of my past. What has happened, has happened. What was, was, and will be forever more. It's over. It's done. It's ancient history. I accept it as immutable. There is no reason to ever again be hurt by thoughts of that changeless past event. It's time to move on. I know I can't change what happened to me. However, I know I can change how I think about what happened to me. Bring on the *SOAP!*

7. *I alone give feelings to the memories of feelingless past events.*

Past events are just past events; that's all they are. They have no feelings in and of themselves. It is the thoughts which I dwell upon about a past event that cause my feelings about that event. I know I possess the power to control my thought dwelling. Therefore, I possess the power to control my feelings. By refusing to dwell upon a Satan-I negative thought about a past event, I am choosing to eliminate all negative feelings about what that person did to me. My goal is not to feel positive about what that person did to me. That is a totally unrealistic and unattainable goal. My goal is to feel neutral about the event. My goal is to make what that person did to me an historical event only, virtually void of all feeling. I can and will accomplish this goal.

8. *Good people and children of God don't hate other people.*

I do not want to be consumed with hate for anyone. I do not think of myself as a hateful person. I am not that kind of person. I am a good person. I know that good people don't hate other people. I know children of God do not hate other people. Therefore, I forsake hate because I am a good person and a child of God.

9. *It is to my physical and mental benefit to stop hating another person.*

I know that when I hate someone, I do not hurt the person I hate. I am the only person I hurt. I hurt myself physically and mentally. I do not want to hurt myself. That is foolish. Therefore, a very sound reason for ceasing to hate another person is to heal myself. It's time to give up hate. I want to heal myself. I shall heal myself. It's time to get on with God's work.

10. *I know it is impossible for me to have enduring peace of mind so long as I hate one human being.*

If I continue to harbor hate, I can never have enduring peace of mind. I can never have the good life. I choose to SOAP away those Satan-I negative thoughts of hate for a very selfish reason, so that I can possess inner peace, enduring peace of mind, God's contentment, the good life.

11. *My hate has become rotten; it is time to dispose of it.*

Hate is a very personal thing. My hate is my hate. It doesn't belong to anyone else. I own it. Unfortunately for me, it is like owning rotten garbage. I do not want to own rotten garbage. It sickens me. I do not want to own hate. It also sickens me. I give my rotten garbage to the garbage man to dispose of. I give my hate to God to dispose of.

12. *I begin to abolish my hate by praying for the person I hate.*

Concerning this person for whom I harbor ill feelings, I know I must daily pray that he or she has enduring peace of mind. Unless I do that, I will never have enduring peace of mind. I promise from this day forward I will daily pray that my transgressor may enjoy enduring peace of mind. No matter how much it hurts me, I will make this daily prayer. It is God's plan. I will follow God's plan. I understand the awesome ramifications of "Forgive me my trespasses as I forgive those who trespass against me."

13. *Regardless of what that person did to me, there is a reasonable time limit to how long I should feel powerless, worthless, seek pity from others, or indulge in self-pity.*

Because of the combination of what was done to me and my negative thinking, I may *choose* to feel powerless, worthless, seek pity from others, or indulge in self-pity. How long I *choose* to feel that way is entirely up to me. If I am wise, the time period is relatively short. I should not hurt myself for a long period of time. I fully accept and now set for myself a recovery time, *a specific date* that I deem reasonable, after which I will no longer feel powerless, worthless, seek pity from others, or indulge in self-pity because of what that person did to me. I choose to do that. I can do that. I will do that. It is reasonable that I should stop hating the person on or before *(date)*, or within (1 year, 5 years, 10 years).

If I refuse to pick a date it is because I still desire the pity of others, or I desire to indulge in my own Satan-I self-pity. I shall cease being a pity seeker! My date is_____.

14. *In working through my healing, I must never attempt to Obliterate all thoughts of what that person did to me.*

Concerning what that person did to me, I promise not to try to SOAP away *all* memories of the event and act as if it never happened. It is impossible and foolhardy to even try to do so. Further, it would be very harmful to me to try to sweep under some mental rug *all* the thoughts of what the person did to me. The thoughts are there. *They must be dealt with.* It is how I deal with the thoughts of the event that is important.

15. *My Satan-I wants to own my mind and then my soul. He fills my mind with negative thoughts to prevent my healing.*

Satan-I will do everything he can to prevent me from possessing enduring peace of mind. It is natural for that to occur. I expect it to occur. That is Satan-I's quest.

Satan-I most definitely does not want me to forgive the person who offended me. My Satan-I wants me to hate that person forever. To make me continue to hate my transgressor, my Satan-I will attempt to make me feel sorry for myself and cause me every possible emotional disturbance by introducing into my mind such thoughts as:

• Why did that happen to me?
• How could he do that to me?

- She has taken away my power to be happy!
- I'll never get over what he did to me!
- I feel so worthless!
- Oh, poor me!
- Anyone, please pity me!
- I feel so sorry for myself!
- I hate him! I hate him! I hate him!
- I can never forgive her! Nobody could forgive her!

When such thoughts come into my mind, I solemnly promise myself that I will *habitually* and immediately Stop, Obliterate, Alter, Praise. *There will never be an exception.* I take full responsibility for my ill feelings resulting from my continuing to dwell upon such Satan-I negative thoughts. I will never again dwell upon such thoughts. Thank God for **SOAP**!

16. *My God-I fills my mind with self-enriching, self-healing thoughts to assist me in my healing.*

    It is characteristic of God-I to fill my mind with thoughts of forgiveness. It is natural for that to happen. I expect it to happen. This is assistance by my God-I to get me over the bad memories of what that person did to me. My God-I very much desires that I have enduring peace of mind. These are the God-I thoughts I will dwell upon to regain my enduring peace of mind:

- Life on this earth is far from perfect. It is being with God that is perfect. If I want to enjoy the next life with God, I must become God-like in this life. I forgive my enemy to get to the perfect life.

- People can really be mean and vicious. Actually, I feel sorry for mean and vicious people.

- I haven't been singled out to be hurt by another person. It happens to everyone. It is part of the human experience. It is Satan working in other people.

- What happened to me happened to a lot of people. The wise people have overcome it. They are at peace. I can deal with it. I can be where they are. I can be at peace.

- What happened to me wasn't nearly as bad as what happened to other people who made peace with their pasts. When I start to feel sorry for myself, I should compare what someone did to me with what has happened to other people. This includes being seriously maimed or crippled by hoodlums, gang raped, having eyes plucked out, being doused with gasoline and set ablaze, or witnessing the brutal murdering of one's entire family. Yet many of those people do not feel sorry for themselves. They have made peace with their pasts. That gives me incredible hope. If they did it, I can do it!

- What happened to me could have been a lot worse. In a sense, I'm blessed that nothing more happened to me. Thank God it wasn't worse!

- I know God dwells within me. I know I have the magnificent Power of God at the center of my being. I can draw upon this Power to overcome the Satan-I memories of what that person did to me. I shall immediately start to draw upon that Power, whereby I will be healed.

- God and I together are infinitely stronger than Satan. All I have to do is believe and ask and God will give me the Power to vanquish the Other People Dragon.

- I alone am responsible for how I feel every conscious moment of my life

I promise myself that I will *only* dwell upon the above type God-I positive thoughts in working through my healing. That is precisely what God wants me to do. For my own well-being, I shall do it.

17. *In working through my healing, I must fiercely control when I do and do not think about what that person did to me.*

What I promise myself is that I will exercise rigid self-discipline over my thought dwelling about the event in question. I promise that I will never think about what that person did to me in terms of Satan-I negative thoughts.
I promise myself I will use Stop, Obliterate, Alter, Praise every time I experience a Satan-I negative thought about what the person did to me—Healing Step 15 type thoughts. I may have to say Stop, Obliterate, Alter, Praise, over and over again to rid myself of Satan-I negative stinking-thinking about the event, but I will do whatever is necessary to stop stinking-thinking.

I promise myself I will only dwell upon God-I healing thoughts about the event—Healing Step 16 type thoughts. I promise God-I and myself that I will never consciously violate this rule. That is how I draw upon the mighty Power at the center of my being to slay the Other People Dragon. By only dwelling upon God-I positive thoughts about the event, I am invincible against the Other People Dragon.

18. *I know I am healed when I can think about the event in historical thoughts only, with virtually no emotional impact.*

It is not my goal to ever feel positive about what that person did to me. That would be bizarre and is totally unrealistic. My goal is to be healed of the mental wounds inflicted on me by the other person.

I know I have overcome the crippling effects of the memory of what that person did to me when I can think about him or her and the event and it no longer has a debilitating emotional impact on me. The once highly emotionally disturbing memories of the event become nothing more than memories of an historical event virtually void of emotion. When I can say, *without emotion*, "What has happened, has happened," then I am healed.

19. *Everything has its price. That is especially true when it comes to possessing enduring peace of mind.*

I will repeat the Healing Steps over and over again, a thousand times if necessary, until the memory of what that person did to me becomes nothing more than the memory of an historical event. Then I have slain the Other People Dragon. Then I have won.

20. *I am triumphant. I am the victor. I have taken complete control of my thought dwelling.*

I now know with absolute certainty that no person, not even my Satan-I, can destroy my enduring peace of mind unless *I* allow it. I choose not to allow it. I can disallow it since, with the God strength within me, I am the master of my thought dwelling!

21. *At last, what was my negative past has become nonexistent, immutable, and feelingless! I am truly free!*

Then you end with a line from a prayer that Eileen created, and that we try to recite every morning, "Please dear God, let me live only in the present and plan for the future."

There you have it. You have become Luminary Mary, Wise David, Victor Frankl, and Adeline Hider all rolled into one very positive person. No matter what anyone did to you in your past, now you say with great joy, "It really doesn't matter. That's just a dead, feelingless, past event. That person and Satan-I no longer have any control over me. I seldom think about what that person did to me. Why would I? If I continue to think about that event, it is because I am seeking pity. I certainly don't need anyone else's pity. I certainly don't desire to wallow in my own self-pity. When

Satan-I shoots a negative thought about the event into my mind, I unemotionally SOAP it away. The thought of the event no longer has an emotional impact on me. Farewell forever Satan-I negative feelings. Farewell forever stinking-thinking. Farewell forever the Other People Dragon. Go-back-to-hell-Satan-I."

My cohorts and loving critics, Marvelous Marvin Brown, Bill Newman, and Paul Salvadori, believe a summary of the Healing Steps, without the individual texts, would be very helpful to you for a quick reference when it is necessary for you to confront the Other People Dragon. Because of the tremendous respect I have for the opinions of those brothers in Christ, I provide the following summary. I trust it will be of value to you when you next confront the despicable Other People Dragon:

1. I accept the fact that I am not singled out for trauma caused by other people.
2. I must get my traumatic incident and recovery into proper perspective.
3. Without God, I admit I am powerless against Satan in the form of the Other People Dragon.
4. To be healed from the negative memories of what another person did to me means that I am willing to take full responsibility for how I feel in the present moment.
5. What another person did to me is a dead event that can no longer hurt me.
6. What another person did to me is a changeless event. I should not be disturbed by thoughts of a changeless event.
7. I alone give feelings to the memories of feelingless past events.
8. Good people and children of God don't hate other people.
9. It is to my physical and mental benefit to stop hating another person.
10. I know it is impossible for me to have enduring peace of mind so long as I hate one human being.
11. My hate has become rotten; it is time to dispose of it.

12. I begin to abolish my hate by praying for the person I hate.

13. Regardless of what that person did to me, there is a reasonable time limit to how long I should feel powerless, worthless, seek pity from others, or indulge in self-pity.

14. In working through my healing, I must never attempt to Obliterate all thoughts of what that person did to me.

15. My Satan-I wants to own my mind and then my soul. He fills my mind with negative thoughts to prevent my healing.

16. My God-I fills my mind with self-enriching, self-healing thoughts to assist me in my healing.

17. In working through my healing, I must fiercely control when I do and do not think about what that person did to me.

18. I know I am healed when I can think about the event in historical thoughts only, with virtually no emotional impact.

19. Everything has its price. That is especially true when it comes to possessing enduring peace of mind.

20. I am triumphant. I am the victor. I have taken complete control of my thought dwelling.

21. At last, what was my negative past has become nonexistent, immutable, and feelingless! I am truly free!

I pray that you forever fully feel God's peace that already exists at the center of your being.

Postscript

The question is often asked, "*Why* do people do bad things to us?" Clearly, that question is outside the scope of this book.

My personal belief is that people do bad things to us for many different reasons. Those include, but are not limited to envy, anger, covetousness, jealousy, resentment, hate, greed, lust, and rivalry. By succumbing to their Satan-I *nature*, some people are *naturally* cruel and vicious.

It is very important that you do not waste your valuable present moment fretting over *why* people do what they do to you. That is just another of Satan-I's ploys to destroy your enduring peace of mind.

For the purpose of our discussion, it is not important *why* people do what they do to us. What is important is that we learn how to swiftly deal with the unavoidable injustices perpetrated by others that occur in our lives.

Synopsis

Say to yourself:

What a happy, beautiful, and joyous day this is! This is the day I slew the Other People Dragon. It is the day I overpowered my worst enemy, Satan-I! At last, I unleashed the God given awesome Power within me to rid myself of any and all emotional baggage that I have carried as a result of what another person did to me in my past. I know what that person did to me has absolutely nothing to do with how I feel in the present moment. I control my feelings by controlling my thought dwelling. I choose not to let Satan-I negative thoughts of what he or she did to me drag me down, to destroy my enduring peace of mind. I know that I alone am responsible for how I feel every conscious moment of my life. I freely make the magnificent choice to accept total responsibility for my feelings. I make the divine choice to forgive and pray for anyone who hurt me. I choose to no longer blame any other person for my feelings. I choose enduring peace of mind. I choose to complete my good-life puzzle. I choose to live only in the present and plan for the future. I revel in knowing these choices are clearly mine to make. Never again will I make the horrible mistake of letting what happened in one of my yesterdays destroy the peace of my today. I choose to be forever *free* from emotionally negative thoughts about what another person did to me in my past. Hallelujah!

Good Life Truths
Derived from Chapter Nine

9-1.   It is not at all important what another person did to me in my past. It is most important what thoughts I dwell upon relating to what that person did to me in my past.

9-2.   I alone am responsible for how I feel every conscious moment of my life, regardless of the injustices other people perpetrated upon me in my past.

9-3.   When I hate someone, I do not hurt the person I hate, I only hurt myself.

9-4.   When I feel angry about what that person did to me, I must admit that I am allowing Satan-I negative thoughts of my nonexistent, immutable, and feelingless past to interfere with my present moment peace of mind.

9-5.   In working my way through my healing, I use Stop, Obliterate, Alter, Praise when I experience Satan-I negative thoughts about the event or person. I deliberately *only* dwell upon God-I positive thoughts about the event or person. By doing that, I work through my hurt, I *deal* with the hurt. I get it *behind* me. I get on *with* my life. I *slay* the Other People Dragon! I am the victor!

CHAPTER TEN

FORGIVING YOURSELF FOR YOUR PAST MISTAKES

It is time to confront and slay Satan's second fire breathing dragon that stands in the way of making peace with our pasts, the infernal Me Dragon.

I am convinced that the Me Dragon is the most ferocious and vicious of the three dragons. But no matter how ferocious and vicious, we are well armed to confront and slay this loathsome beast.

The Dual Battle Plans of the Me Dragon

What makes the Me Dragon especially dangerous is his ability to attack us head on and his ability to mount a rearward assault.

When he confronts us head on, it is in the form of making us think and believe that we are not responsible for our past mistakes. Someone else or something outside of our control is responsible for our past mistakes. In the frontal attack, the Me Dragon gets us into a state of mind whereby we completely refuse to accept responsibility for our past actions. I call that state of mind the "blame another person" or "it's not my fault" state of mind.

If the frontal attack fails, the Me Dragon whirls around us and mounts an attack from the rear. A reverse attack is just the opposite of a frontal attack. It takes the form of our being obsessed with our past mistakes. It is the state of mind whereby we refuse to ever forgive ourselves for what we did. I call this state of mind the "blame myself" or "it's all my fault" state of mind.

Let us examine the two war plans of the Me Dragon, the "blame another person/it's not my fault" state of mind, and the "blame myself/it's all my fault" state of mind. Both of those are very dangerous states of mind.

Accepting Our Fallibility and Personal Responsibility

Let us first confront the Me Dragon when he gets us into the state of believing that we are not responsible for our past mistakes, the blame another person/it's not my fault state of mind.

When in this state of mind, we commence our quest of overcoming and slaying the Me Dragon with the simple realization that we can never come to peace with our pasts until we do accept total responsibility for our past actions.

If you are unwilling to accept responsibility for your past mistakes, your Me Dragon has you in a blame another person/it's not my fault state of mind. In that state of mind, you find something or someone else to *blame* for that stupid mistake *you* made. You say, "It certainly wasn't my fault. It's all *his* fault!" Despite the fact *you* made the mistake, it is without exception something or someone else's fault. In this blame state of mind, you will always feel like a victim.

If Satan-I can keep you in the blame another person/it's not my fault state of mind, you will invariably find something or someone else to *blame* for every past mistake you ever made. Then Satan-I wins and you lose big time. As long as you are in that state of mind, it will be impossible for you to have peace in the present moment. You will always be stubbornly parked under your cherry tree with life seeming very unpleasant to you. You will never over-come negative feelings caused by negative thought dwelling. *Plop. Plop. Plop.*

When it comes to past mistakes, our goal is to maintain a God-I state of mind. A God-I state of mind is unequivocally accepting with unquestioning conviction that we are human, that we err, and that no other person or thing is to *blame* for our mistakes but us.

We create a God-I state of mind by saying: "I unequivocally accept with unquestioning conviction that I am human, that I err and that no other person or thing is to *blame* for my mistakes but me!" Say it once again. Now say:

"I alone am responsible for cheating, stealing, drinking, dop-ing, lying, lusting, and gossiping. No one is to blame, but me.

"I alone voluntarily committed adultery. No one is to blame, but me."

"I alone am responsible for that unlawful killing I committed. No one is to blame, but me."

"I alone am responsible for the domestic violence I perpetrated against my family. No one is to blame, but me."

"I alone am responsible for every thing I do. No one is to blame for my choices, but me. My choices, no matter how stupid, are my choices."

That is what accountability is all about. Being accountable means accepting the fact that when you make stupid mistakes you acknowledge that *you* erred. You never look for something or some-one else to blame for *your* mistakes. You hold yourself account-able. You readily admit *your* mistakes.

When you accept total responsibility for your acts and the natu-ral consequences that flow therefrom, then the healing process commences. God will reward you with enduring peace of mind once you accept a healthy responsibility for your past acts.

Many people are not willing to accept that responsibility.

Lyle the Blamer

Lyle is a high school graduate with one semester of college. In a trial over which I presided, a jury convicted him of possessing for the purpose of selling a controlled substance, namely, methamphetamine.

Although his record was not particularly significant, it was clear that Lyle was a recidivist and was becoming a danger to the community. Therefore, I sentenced him to the maximum term of four years in the California Department of Corrections. With good time credit, he'll only serve one-half of that time. Lyle will be back on the streets in two years.

When it came his turn to speak at his sentencing, Lyle the Blamer *blamed* his plight on everyone but himself.

"Those pig cops had no right to break into my house. You know their search warrant was no damn good. (It was a valid search warrant.) And what right did they have to confiscate those scales and baggies? I told them those things weren't mine. Some dude who used to live with us left them there."

No one escaped his scourge. "How about this character you appointed as my attorney? I would have been better off without him. You should have let me represent myself." (He had one of the best public defenders in our county.)

Spitting more venom, he continued, "And you call that jury a jury of my peers? What do they know about dope and selling dope? What do they know about anything? They've never been there. They've never done that. I've used marijuana every day since I was ten years old. At twelve, I began using methamphetamine. I'm hooked on 'crack'. I've been free-basing it since I was fifteen years old. I've used heroin, PCP, angel dust, sherm, and wack. What the hell do any of you know about this stuff?"

The tirade went on to a point of being insufferable. I ordered that Lyle the Blamer be removed from the proceedings. Two bailiffs literally wrestled a handcuffed, ankle chained, kicking and screaming Lyle out of my courtroom. I will always remember his parting ventilation, "You sons of..., I'll get all of you."

I am confident Lyle the Blamer will suffer discontentment for a long period of time. He doesn't have a clue that in order to make peace with his past, he must begin by accepting responsibility for his past mistakes and the consequences that naturally flow from those mistakes.

Hopefully a prison chaplain can lead Lyle the Blamer down the path of accepting responsibility for his acts. That in turn will lead to personal accountability. But for the present time, Lyle finds it necessary to *blame* something or someone else for his arrest, conviction, and sentence. As we know, he is wrong.

Lyle the Blamer is pigheadedly parked under his cherry tree. No matter how illogical his position, he refuses to remove his foot from the brake pedal of blaming other people for his ill feelings. He is a chronic victim. Satan-I owns his mind. *Plop. Plop. Plop.*

In contrast:

Learner Luke

Luke is a high school dropout. To support his cocaine habit, he began selling drugs. Unfortunately for Luke, he sold a few rocks of cocaine to an undercover agent. I was able to negotiate a plea bargain whereby he entered a no contest plea to a charge of sale of a controlled substance. As part of the plea bargain, other charges against him were dismissed.

Luke's criminal record started fifteen years earlier. Among other convictions, he had a conviction for participating in an armed robbery. That is a strike under California's Three Strikes Law.

I sentenced Luke to state prison for the upper term of five years for selling cocaine. That was doubled to ten years because of his earlier strike. Also, under the Three Strikes Law, he will have to serve eighty per cent of the sentence. Luke will be in prison for approximately eight years.

Luke was a perfect gentleman throughout the sentencing. Except for himself, he had no one nor anything else to *blame* for his plight. He totally accepted self-responsibility and the consequences of prison that flowed from his acts. As he left the courtroom, he commented: "Judge Hider, I want to thank you for being fair to me. Believe me, I've learned my lesson. You will never see me in your courtroom again."

I gave Luke a few words of encouragement and advised him to make the most out of the time he would spend in prison.

I later received a warm letter from Luke. It reads:

Judge Hider,

Just a quick note to let you know how I'm doing. I'm continuing my education here in prison and have taken up painting, something I always wanted to do. I enclose a small picture I painted for you. I hope you like it.

I want to thank you for what you did for me. Your sentence was fair. Actually, by sending me to prison, you probably saved my life. If I had stayed on the streets much longer, I probably would have killed someone, or been killed myself. I can't believe the stupid things I was doing.

I'm working on my GED. I hope to have it completed by next year. After that, I plan on taking some community college extension courses. This is really exciting to me.

I also found my way back to church. As a boy, my mother would take me to church every Sunday. She died nine years ago today. I sure miss her.

I never knew my dad.

It feels good to be back in church. If I had not stopped going to church, you never would have met me.

Good luck to you and your family. I wish you a very Merry Christmas and a Happy New Year.

God bless you,
Luke Smith

I responded with a reassuring letter and thanked him for the painting, which is hanging on my wall.

Many traumas have come into Learner Luke's life. Not knowing his father, being on the streets, and now in prison for eight years is no picnic. However, Luke finally accepted responsibility for his actions, how he thinks, and how he feels. He accepts God's forgiveness. He forgives himself. God's peace is in him. He is only an historical victim. I doubt he will ever again turn control of his mind over to Satan-I. He has zoomed away from his cherry tree. He is on the road that leads to enduring peace of mind.

Consider the similarities and the differences here. The same judge sentenced Lyle the Blamer and Learner Luke at approximately the same time, to the same prison, and both for drug offenses. Luke will be in prison six years longer than Lyle. Yet, they have antipodal feelings in the present moment. Why? Simply stated, Lyle refuses to accept responsibility for his acts and the consequences that flow therefrom. Luke, on the other hand, accepts total responsibility for his acts and the resulting consequences.

When it comes to accepting responsibility for our past mistakes, we all should be like Luke. Many people are. Many people are not. But some of the latter group eventually arrive at the God-I state of mind of accepting responsibility for their acts. A good example from this latter group is the convicted murderer Sam Huddleston. I encourage you to review Sam's transition from non-acceptance to acceptance of personal responsibility as set forth in Chapter Eight.

We can learn much from spiritual titans like Sam Huddleston. We learn that when we err, taking total responsibility for our mistakes is the very first requirement if we ever hope to kill our Me Dragons, and make peace with our pasts.

If you accept that responsibility, you will no longer *blame* anything or anyone for your past mistakes. You will never again be in the blame another person/it's not my fault state of mind. You move your foot from the brake pedal to the accelerator of your mind. You are about to draw upon the awesome Power within you to pull away from your cherry tree.

Well, Maybe!

Satan-I, in the form of the Me Dragon, doesn't give up that easily.

It is a gross understatement to say that the mind is a very complex entity. If we were not cognizant of the supernatural power of Satan, we would not be able to understand what seems to be a strange phenomenon. Lyle the Blamer, our extremely angry defendant, is a prime example of a person who will not accept responsibility for his mistakes. But there are people at the other end of the spectrum who become obsessed with the thoughts of their past errors. For them, the Me Dragon takes on a rearward assault. That is the blame myself/it's all my fault state of mind. An example:

Defeated Louis

Louis was an entrepreneur I casually knew. He was very successful and acquired much wealth. He had a most loving family who gave him unending support.

In mid-life, Louis's interests turned to politics. He unsuccessfully ran for a Federal political office in three different elections. Satan-I, taking the form of the Me Dragon, attacked from the rear. He convinced Louis, a perfectionist, that he did a horrible job in the manner in which he and his campaign workers conducted those campaigns. Louis could not recover from a Satan-I "it's all my fault" state of mind.

Despite his loving family and wealth, life became intolerable for Defeated Louis. Because of his Satan-I thought dwelling about his losses, and because of his great pride, he *blamed* himself, and could not recover from his political defeats.

Shortly after his third defeat, Louis disjoined his head from his shoulders with a shotgun. Satan-I owned his mind, then his life, and possibly his soul.

Note the Difference in the Me Dragon's Mode of Attack

Do not miss the important difference in the thinking of Lyle the Blamer type people and the thinking of Defeated Louis type people.

Lyle the Blamer is not troubled by his past mistakes because he does not perceive them as mistakes. He is only doing what comes naturally. His acts are acts; that's all they are. He does not associate responsibility with his acts. The concept of accepting responsibility for his acts never occurs to him. In his mind, he is neither legally nor morally responsible for what he does. Cause and effect never occurs to him. When something goes awry, it is because someone else is interfering with his lifestyle. Everyone else is to blame for his present predicament. Lyle the Blamer thinks of himself as a chronic victim of an untoward system that is interfering with his freedom. The Me Dragon attacked and defeated Lyle the Blamer head on. Satan-I owns him.

On the other hand, Louis the Defeated blamed himself for everything that went wrong in his campaigns. He assumed the culpability regardless of who or what was really to blame. Everything that went wrong was his fault alone. He was the cause of *everything* that led to his losing his elections. He not only accepted total responsibility for his mistakes, he eagerly accepted total responsibility for the mistakes of all his campaign workers and whatever else went amiss. The Me Dragon sneaked up behind Louis the Defeated and devoured him without his having a clue about what was occurring.

Obviously, it is absolutely wrong to be as cavalier as Lyle the Blamer about our past mistakes, so that we are unwilling to accept responsibility for any of the consequences that flow therefrom. That is the Me Dragon attacking us head on. On the other hand, it is equally wrong to be so totally obsessed with the thoughts of our past mistakes that it destroys us. That is the Me Dragon attacking us from the rear.

The correct disposition is a state of mind whereby responsibility for one's acts is accepted, but not obsessively.

An excellent example of this correct state of mind, and a startling contrast to Defeated Louis is Richard Milhous Nixon. Nixon personifies the correct state of mind when it comes to accepting past failures. Nixon did not let Satan-I thoughts of past defeats destroy his life. He immediately Obliterated such thoughts. He refused to take "No" for an answer.

Nixon

In 1960, Richard Milhous Nixon ran for President of the United States. John Fitzgerald Kennedy defeated him.

Undaunted, not dwelling on the Me Dragon negative thoughts of defeat, pride, or self-condemnation, Nixon returned to his home state of California and immediately immersed himself in state politics. In 1962, he ran for Governor of California. After spending untold sums of money, much effort and time, he was soundly defeated by Edmund G. (Pat) Brown.

Nixon lost the race for the top office in the nation and lost the race for the top office in California. But without trepidation, and refusing to adopt either of Satan-I's *blaming* states of mind, in 1968 he boldly ran again for President of the United States. This time his quest was fulfilled. He was elected the 37th President of the United States.

Nixon proves that when we Obliterate the Me Dragon's *blame* states of mind, our minds are unfettered and capable of accomplishing almost anything.

It is not surprising that one of President Nixon's more famous quotes is, "A man is not finished when he's defeated; he's finished when he quits."

Turning to Confront the Me Dragon's Rear Assault

We forgive other people for what they did to us. We forgive Fate for what it did to us. But, the act of self-forgiveness seems especially difficult.

As stated earlier, it is my belief that the inability to forgive one's self for one's past mistakes is the most ferocious of the three dragons. The old adage is true, we are our own worst enemies.

Satan-I, in the form of the Me Dragon, loves to get us into an obsessively remorseful state of mind. That state of mind renders us mentally impotent in the present moment. He then owns our minds. That state of mind prevents us from doing the work of God. It can, and often does, lead to suicide.

The Me Dragon revels in bringing to our minds memories of our past mistakes. She is out to plague our minds with as many disturbing thoughts about our mistakes as possible. That is the Me Dragon's goal.

Tell me about your Me Dragon's rearward attacks. Have you ever stolen anything? Sold dope? Cheated on your spouse? Mismanaged a business transaction? Committed a social blunder of incredible proportions? Made a complete fool of yourself? Dropped an expensive heirloom? Stood drunk atop a friend's new car? Put a loaded gun to someone's head to rob him? Negligently killed or seriously injured another person? Murdered anyone? Or, how about this one?

> They threw him [Stephen] out of the city, and began to stone him. The witnesses laid down their cloaks at the feet of a young man named Saul [who God later named Paul]. As they were stoning Stephen, he called out, "Lord Jesus, receive my spirit." Then he fell to his knees and cried out in a loud voice, "Lord, do not hold this sin against them," and when he said this he fell asleep. . . .
> Now Saul was consenting to his execution. . . .
> Saul, meanwhile, was trying to destroy the church; entering house after house and dragging out men and women, he handed them over for imprisonment. (Acts 7:58–8:1,3 NAB)

And later we are told:

> Now Saul, still breathing murderous threats against the disciples of the Lord, went to the high priest and asked him for letters to the synagogues in Damascus, that, if he should find any men or women who belonged to the Way, he might bring them back to Jerusalem in chains. (Acts 9:12 NAB)

Talk about past mistakes! Big mistakes, Saul! Big, big mistakes! Instigating and encouraging the death of a guiltless boy, tantamount to murder. Entering house after house and dragging out innocent men, women, and children to be handed over for imprisonment, torture, and maybe death. With a vengeance, trying to destroy God's Church. Big mistakes!

Was Saul, after he became St. Paul, able to forgive himself for following his murderous ways? Was he at all hindered by his despicable past, or was he able to get his enormous sinfulness behind him and get on with God's work?

It is precisely because of the magnitude of his mistakes and the brilliant slaying of his Me Dragon that I choose St. Paul as our standard-bearer. It is my firmest belief that God clearly set forth the life of St. Paul in the Bible as an example of how we must forgive ourselves for past transgressions. It is God's will that we learn to forgive ourselves for our past mistakes.

Upon his conversion to Christianity, St. Paul *immediately* whirled around and viciously slew his Me Dragon once and for all. Thereafter, he never looked back on his acts of infamy. He refused to allow others to judge him. He refused to judge himself. Although never blaming his past mistakes on anyone else, obsessive remorse was not in his vocabulary. He had no time for obsessive remorse. He abhorred it, just as we must abhor it.

After St. Paul's conversion, he moved on to doing the work of God. We are told:

> He stayed some days with the disciples in Damascus, and he began at once to proclaim Jesus in the synagogues, that he is the Son of God. (Acts 9:19-20 NAB)

And to those who had the audacity to judge him, St. Paul had a stinging message:

> It does not concern me in the least that I be judged by you or any human tribunal; *I do not even pass judgment on myself*; I am not conscious of anything against me, but I do not thereby stand acquitted; the one who judges me is the Lord. (1 Cor. 4:3–4 NAB)

Wow! Talk about forgiving one's self! I could rest my case right here.

In a flash (excuse the pun) St. Paul went from a murderous warrior for Satan to become one of God's most valiant and humble disciples.

It is clear that St. Paul never looked back in a debilitating way on his past mistakes. Nowhere in the Bible is there one scintilla of evidence that St. Paul was ever bothered by obsessive remorse for his past acts. He did not get bogged down with thoughts of his dead, unchangeable, feelingless past. He did exactly what God would have any of us do. He humbly asked for God's forgiveness one time only. He accepted Divine forgiveness. Then, following God's command, he forgave himself and got on with serving God. He refused to be concerned about other people judging him. He didn't care what they thought. Even more important, he *refused* to judge himself! *He simply refused to think about his past in a negative way.* He lived in the present, the here and now, and planned for the future. Sounds like some other wise people we've met.

We can be certain that St. Paul's intrepid assailant, Satan-I, in the form of the Me Dragon, attempted time and again to fill the new Paul's mind with thoughts of self-condemnation, self-accusation, self-reproach, guilt, compunction, or obsessive remorse for the stupid things he did as Saul. But St. Paul would have no part of that. He mightily wielded his sword of Stop, Obliterate, Alter, Praise, and with a vengeance again and again slew his Me Dragon. Self-defeating thoughts were not allowed to remain in his mind. St. Paul made his peace with God; he had no time for Satan-I self-condemnation for his past mistakes.

I can imagine the inimitable St. Paul screaming aloud:

> Where are you hiding Satan-I? Come engage me in battle! I hold the impenetrable shield of knowing that my past is nonexistent, immutable, and feelingless. I brandish the noble and shiny sword of Stop, Obliterate, Alter, Praise. I feel the strength of Almighty God at the center of my being. It is not my strength, but the strength of the Holy Spirit that makes me invincible. Come Satan-I! Come do me battle! I beseech you!

Nothing, but silence. So St. Paul got on with God's work.

If we truly call ourselves children of God, we are bound by the same law to do and act like St. Paul when it comes to our past mistakes. To call ourselves children of God and not to forgive ourselves after God has forgiven us is hypocrisy in its worst form.

There can be no doubt that once St. Paul accepted himself as the temple of the Holy Spirit with God-I as his benefactor, he experienced a joy and contentment he had never before experienced. As Saul, he was filled with hate, anger, rage, and vengeance. Satan owned him. As Paul, he was filled with love and God's peace at the center of his being. Then, Satan-I in the form of his Me Dragon was nowhere to be found in his life.

St. Paul came to realize, as we must come to realize, that peace and contentment derive from knowing that the Supreme Power of the universe forgives us our sins, dwells within each of us, and is available to provide us strength to slay the Me Dragon when he attempts to destroy us by having us dwell upon thoughts of our past stupid mistakes. When we draw upon that Power, Satan-I is rendered impotent. There is no more dwelling on thoughts of an ugly past. The unstoppable Power is unceasingly within us. Those who refuse to draw upon this Force choose to sit under the cherry tree with their past pooping all over them. I fervently pray you are not making that mistake.

God's Forgiveness

Let's talk a little more about God's forgiveness. This is an issue we must settle once and for all.

Most of our stupid mistakes are an offense against God. That would include stealing, robbery, drunkenness, using controlled substances, spreading vicious gossip, lust, fornication, domestic violence, adultery, rape, unlawfully killing another person, etc. God considers those acts as sin. He orders us to repent of our sins. Unless we repent, we will never slay the Me Dragon. Satan will forever own our minds. If we do repent, the reward is overwhelming!

When it comes to forgiveness, we start with the realization that no matter how grievous a thing we did, intentionally or negligently, God forgives us the nanosecond we request forgiveness. That is part of God's very nature. God holds no grudges. No mistake is too great for God to forgive. Not persecuting His Church, not murder, not sodomy, not abortion, not rape, not adultery, not selling illegal drugs, not kleptomania, not leading others to sin, not anything. The moment we repent of our wrong, God forgives us our transgression. God has *guaranteed* this!

> If we confess our sins, He is faithful and just to forgive us our sins and to cleanse us from all unrighteousness. (1 John 1:9 NKJV)

> But You have lovingly delivered my soul from the pit of corruption, For You have cast all my sins behind Your back. (Isa. 38:17 NKJV)

> For I will be merciful to their unrighteousness, and their sins and their lawless deeds I will remember no more. (Heb. 8:12 NKJV)

Imagine, Almighty God is willing to cleanse us from *every* wrongdoing and will cast all our sins behind His back! God Himself is telling us He forgives all our transgressions and treats them as if He no longer sees nor cares about them. In fact, He goes further. He promises to not even remember our wrongs. Wow! What a Great God.

Alright, if God isn't going to remember your wrongs, who are you not to forgive yourself? Why are you so upset about your past mistakes? Are your standards higher than God's standards? I pray not.

But wait, God enhances His admonition. He goes on and *orders* us not to condemn ourselves:

> My son, with humility have self-esteem;
> prize yourself as you deserve.
> Who will acquit him who condemns himself?
> who will honor him who discredits himself?
> [The inference is obvious.]
> (Sirach 10:27–28 NAB)

Happy the man whose mouth brings him no grief,
who is not stung by remorse for sin.
Happy the man whose conscience does not reproach him,
who has not lost hope.
(Sirach 14:12 NAB)

As we know, St. Paul was not stung by obsessive remorse. By all accounts in the Bible, he humbly asked God's forgiveness only once. It is God's will that we do the same thing. To keep returning and seeking God's forgiveness over and over again for a particular past mistake is to disrespect God and treat His forgiveness with dishonor.

I can imagine a conversation between Henry, a good Catholic gentleman, and God. Henry confesses his sins and makes a genuine Act of Contrition.

Henry: "Oh my God, I am so heartily sorry for having offended Thee. I detest all my sins because they displease Thee Who art good and deserving of all my love. I firmly resolve, with the help of Thy grace, to confess my sins, to do penance, and to amend my life. Amen."

God: "Henry, I know you are heartily sorry for that offense and I forgive you for sinning just as I forgave my disciple Paul for all of his sins. Now, please do what Paul did and be on with My work. Set an example for all you meet so more souls are snatched away from the grasp of Satan."

A week later, Henry is back on his knees, again begging God for forgiveness for the same offense.

Henry: "God, I am so, so sorry for that sin I committed. Please, please forgive me."

God: "Henry, I told you a week ago that I forgave you that offense. Please, please get on with my work. There is so much to be done."

A month, a year, ten years later:

Henry: "Oh, God, please, please, forgive me that past sin."

God: "Henry, my dear Henry! Did I not tell you I forgave you that sin and that, through the blood of my Son, I cleansed you from *every* wrongdoing? Did I not tell you that I cast behind my back *all* your sins? Did I not tell you I forgave you your evildoing and that I remembered your sins no more? Did I not tell you that with humility you are to have self-esteem? Did I not tell you, 'Happy the man whose conscience does not reproach him, who has not lost hope'?

"Henry, my dearest Henry, why do you continue to refuse to believe my word? Why do you continue to torture yourself? Do you not see this obsessive remorse is Satan's ploy? By being obsessively remorseful, Satan-I keeps you in a blame myself state of mind. He is keeping you from doing My work. Do not waste this irreplaceable precious moment, this now, grieving over dead, past wrongs that I no longer even remember. SOAP away such Satan-I self- defeating thoughts!

"Henry, I have set you free. Now, you must set yourself free.

"Please, please get on with My work. You do not have much time left."

St. Paul understood God's teachings. So you must come to understand God's teachings. If you confessed them, God forgave every sin you ever committed once and for all! Now, you must forgive yourself. It is sinful not to forgive yourself.

However, do not allow Satan-I to cause you to confuse two totally different concepts. It is one thing to be obsessively remorseful over a past sin that God has unequivocally forgiven once and for all. Obsessive remorsefulness is a ploy of Satan-I and very unhealthy.

On the other hand, it is quite another thing to understand that we have a sinful nature because of Satan-I dwelling within each of us. That sinful nature causes us to lash out at family members, friends, and fellow-employees. It causes us to steal, cheat, and lie. It is a very healthy state of mind to recognize our evil nature and to realize it is only by totally relying on God's strength that we can overcome our Satan-I sinful nature.

Therefore, our prayer should not be a constant repetition of "God, please forgive me this sin," ad nauseam. Rather, our prayer should be:

> "Good and Holy God, I call to mind not any of my past sins that I confessed and I know You already forgave. Instead I call to mind my sinful nature. Please provide me with the strength to overcome my sinful nature. Help me to SOAP away every Satan-I, self-defeating, negative thought that enters my mind. Without Your strength to draw upon, I am powerless against Satan-I. He will do with me as he pleases. With Your strength, I am invincible against Satan-I. Please, Dear God, never withdraw Your strength from me. Never abandon me. Let me forever feel Your presence at the center of my being. I beg this in Jesus' name. Amen."

Why?

There is no question that obsessively dwelling upon thoughts of past mistakes is a serious problem for many people. Several of my friends grievously suffer from this malady.

You rightly ask, "Why are so many people unable to forgive themselves for their past mistakes?"

We know Satan is at the root of the problem. He wants us to despise ourselves for our past wrongs. He very much wants to get us into a blame myself state of mind whereby we vehemently hate ourselves. Satan wants to destroy all enduring peace of mind. We know that Satan wants to own our minds, then our souls. One of the ways Satan accomplishes this goal is by taking on the form of the Me Dragon. When we are in a state of self-hate, we are Satan's plaything.

You say, "I realize Satan is at the root of the problem. But what weapons does he use, which cause us not to forgive ourselves for our past mistakes?"

I believe Satan employs many different weapons to keep us in a state of obsessive remorse so that we cannot enjoy enduring peace of mind. Depending on our individual propensity, he selects the arrow to which we are each most vulnerable.

One of Satan's greatest weapons is the arrow of excess pride. The Bible says much about the horrible capital sin of excess pride. The Me Dragon revels in pride, in our excess pride. He wants us to believe we are infallible and that we are incapable of ever doing anything stupid. But, as long as we live in this imperfect world, as long as we possess this worldly mind, we will do stupid things. To err is human. To forgive is divine. It is Satan-I pride that prevents us from being divine, from forgiving ourselves when we do err.

If we put on the full armor of God, we can deflect Satan's arrows of excess pride. If we are not so armored, Satan will pierce us through time and again with those arrows. In the former case, we will maintain our contentment regardless of our past poor judgment, but not so in the latter case.

Concerning pride and humility, the Bible says:

> Humble yourself the more, the greater you are,
> and you will find favor with God.
> For great is the Power of God;
> by the humble he is glorified. . . .
> (Sirach 3:18–19 NAB)

This is a Mother Teresa God-I state of mind that we all should covet and work toward.

> For the affliction of the proud man there is no cure;
> he is the offshoot of an evil plant.
> (Sirach 4:27–28 NAB).

This is a Defeated Louis Satan-I state of mind that we all should despise and avoid at all costs.

And James tells us:

> God resists the proud, But gives grace to the humble. Therefore, submit to God. Resist the devil [Satan-I], and he will flee from you. Draw near to God [God-I], and He will draw near to you. (James 4:67 NKJV).

Of course, Satan has many other arrows besides excess pride to keep us from forgiving ourselves for our past mistakes.

For many people it is the arrow of low self-esteem. No one should forgive us for our mistakes, especially ourselves. We are not worthy of forgiveness! Not from any one, including God, despite what He tells us. How sad.

For other people, it is being pierced with Satan's arrow of *unrealistic* expectations. This arrow is especially effective against the intelligentsia. We expect to be perfect. When we do something we never thought we would do, it is unforgivable.

There are undoubtedly many more arrows in Satan's quiver, which he uses to prevent people from forgiving themselves for their past mistakes. But, I leave further discussion of *why* to the psychiatrist's, psychologist's, and theologians.

It is not nearly as important to know *why* you cannot forgive yourself as it is to know *how* to forgive yourself for your past mistakes. But, before we get to the Healing Steps, there is another matter we must comprehend, which is the foundation upon which the Healing Steps are built.

Separating Who We Are from What We Did

It is important that we learn to separate who we are from what we did.

Early on, we discussed Integrated-I when we referred to any of us individually. That *I* is who *you* are at any given moment. That is the integration of your entire past, your present perception of yourself, the habits of your mind, and your hopes and anxieties about your future. The *you* is in a constant state of flux. You ride the knife-edge crest of your own individual time wave that moves from your past, through the present, to your future. The crest of the time wave is the present moment. It is all that really exists. Your past is behind you. Your future is before you. The older you get, the longer is the portion of the wave behind you and the shorter is the portion of the wave before you.

Past   Present   Future

Moment

The *you* who rides the crest is certainly different from the non-existent *you* who made some stupid mistake in your past. The *you* of this present moment, reading this book, *cannot* be the same person who made that stupid past mistake some time ago. We change every single moment of our lives.

As you know, your mistakes are nonexistent, immutable, and feelingless. They only exist in your mind. You certainly are not nonexistent, immutable, and feelingless. You do not exist only in your mind. Very much to the contrary, you exist, you change, you grow, you are productive, and you know how to control your feelings and perception of yourself by using SOAP to control your thought dwelling.

Further, wise people use their past mistakes as learning experiences. Some of the most valuable things we learn are the product of our past mistakes.

Our attitude should be, "Yes, I made a big mistake in the past. But, I am not that mistake. That is not who I am in the present moment. I learned much from that mistake. I certainly am now much wiser having learned from that past mistake."

No matter what horrendous thing they did, many people, like St. Paul, are able to successfully separate who they are from that terrible thing they did. Those people should be an encouragement to us.

Let me tell you about Martha.

Martha the Absolved

Martha is a health care professional with an impeccable reputation. On a Friday evening, after a long week's work, she attended a peer's retirement party. Usually, she was a nondrinker of alcoholic beverages. However, at the party she drank just enough alcoholic punch to raise her blood alcohol level to the California illegal limit of 0.08 per cent.

On her way home, due to her weariness and the effect of the alchohol, Martha fell asleep and her car pulled into oncoming traffic. A horrendous collision occurred. She killed two teenage boys in a small car. Both boys were excellent students, participated in school sports, active in the community, and very popular.

Since there was no specific criminal intent on her part, Martha was charged with two counts of vehicular manslaughter. The matter came to me for a jury trial. However, I was successful in hammering out a plea bargin between the District Attorney and Martha's attorney, thus avoiding a lengthy and expensive trial.

Under the provisions of the plea bargain, Martha was to receive six months jail time. She would be allowed work furlough during the day, she would report to the jail for custody each evening and weekends, and she would do many hours of community service following her six-month incarceration. But, she would avoid state prison. In addition, she or her insurance company made complete restitution for all expenses incurred by the victims' respective families as a result of the tragic mishap.

Our probation department recommended that I follow the plea bargain.

At Martha's sentencing, the families of the two victims came forward and delivered moving orations. The loss to both families was genuine. As each family member spoke of the excruciating injury and pain he or she felt resulting from those deaths, the audience (including my bailiff, clerk, court reporter, and me) was moved to tears. Family and friends were infuriated that this horrible drunk driver who snuffed out two young, innocent lives was not going to prison for a long period of time, if not the rest of her life.

One of the boys was an only child. His mother spoke for herself and her husband who was not able to speak about the death of his son:

"I thought much about what I would say today. I am trying not to be bitter. But it is very difficult not to be bitter. Charlie was a wonderful boy. We loved him very much. He was a tremendous joy to the entire family. He will be sorely missed. His grandparents are emotionally devastated. They wanted to be here, but decided they could not stand the pain.

"I haven't cleaned out his room yet. I'm not sure I ever will. I suppose I should give his clothes to some needy boys instead of just letting them hang in his closet. But his clothes remind me of him, and I need that for a while longer.

"I said his room, his closet, and his clothes, didn't I? I guess they're still his. I often speak about Charlie as if he's still alive. But he's not alive, is he?

"Martha, I want you to know what I think about all the time. I think about Charlie graduating from high school in the spring. I think about him going on to college. I think about him meeting a nice Christian girl we would accept as the daughter we never had. And I especially think of the grandchildren we will never have. You know, I took all of this for granted, especially that someday we would be grandparents. But now that will never happen. I pray that I never take anything for granted again.

"God, I miss Charlie so much!"

Charlie's mother was unable to continue. Her husband helped her back to her seat.

Martha sat motionlessly throughout all their allocutions. She wept quietly.

Of course, Martha had her defenders. Her family and many professional men and women, pillars of our community, came forward with moving praises for all that Martha had done for the community, which was much.

Martha's husband spoke before she spoke. "Judge Hider, I know the plea bargain calls for six months jail time for Martha. But putting her in a jail cell is not going to accomplish anything.

"This was a most tragic and stupid *accident*. It was a horrible *accident*. But that's what it was, an *accident*, nothing more, nothing less.

"Nothing anyone can do will bring those two boys back to life. Martha did not intentionally harm them. Martha would never intentionally harm anyone. She is a warm, kind, and loving person.

"I beg you not to impose any jail time. What good can it possibly do to have Martha sitting in a cell every night and weekends for six months doing nothing? Instead of imposing jail time, I beg you to increase her community service obligation by doubling the number of hours she would be sitting in jail. That way she can at least be out doing something useful for the community instead of wasting all that precious time.

"Martha has extraordinary talents that can be put to good use helping the needy. She has a special gift. Why not use her talents productively? She's willing to work forty hours per week at her regular job and do an additional forty hours per week in community services by working every evening and weekends. She can't do that if she's in jail. What good does it do anyone to have Martha sit idly in a jail cell? I beg you to be reasonable!"

When it came Martha's time to speak, she made an articulate and impassioned plea for the victims' families to forgive her for her stupid wrong. She made absolutely no attempt to avoid responsibility for her acts. She unashamedly begged God's forgiveness. She now sought their forgiveness. She lovingly reminded them of Alexander Pope's assertion, "To err is human; to forgive is divine."

Unfortunately, her plea fell on ears of stone.

As has happened many times during my years on the bench, I could empathize with both sides, and I told them so.

"If Charlie had been my only child, . . ."

"If I made the stupid mistake that Martha made, . . ."

I approved the plea bargain and sentenced Martha to the agreed upon jail time and agreed upon hours of community service. Martha has served her jail time. She is now going to our middle and high schools lecturing on the evil consequences of drinking and driving. I pray she is able to dissuade some young people from drinking and driving, from erring as she erred. I know it is doing Martha much good. She no longer drinks alcoholic beverages. She has also pledged her life to continuing her campaign against drinking and driving and to better our community in any manner she can.

Like St. Paul, Martha has forgiven herself for what she did. She had to, in order to survive, to be a productive citizen, and to do God's work. She is carrying on with her life in a better direction, with new goals, and living closer to God. She is clearly doing God's work. Out of much tragedy she brought much good. In a sense, she is a modern day Paul the Apostle.

Martha has personally come to realize the enormous love God has for each of us, regardless of the stupid things we each have done in our respective pasts. By giving part of Himself to each of us, He empowers us with inconceivable Power. More than enough Power to forgive our past follies. More than enough Power to forever crush Satan-I negative stinking-thinking about our past mistakes.

Most unfortunately, not all of us are as wise as St. Paul and Martha. Because of dwelling on Satan-I negative thoughts about past errors, many of us are blinded to the tremendous Power of God within us. Stan is one of these persons.

Despondent Stan

As a juvenile, Stan had a series of minor criminal offenses. As an adult, he graduated into drug use, and finally attempted a lewd and lascivious act with a minor. He was tried and convicted. I sentenced him to state prison for sixteen months. With good time and work time credits, he was to be out of prison in eight months.

At his sentencing, it was obvious Stan was obsessively remorseful for his stupid act. He could not forgive himself for his escalating criminal behavior, especially his last act of attempted sexual molestation. Stan clearly manifested that the Me Dragon controlled his mind. I knew he was in trouble.

While in prison, Stan unsuccessfully tried suicide by cutting his wrists, and later by hanging. He was transferred to a California State hospital. While there, he made a suicide attempt by jumping off a forty-foot high roof. Stan is now a quadriplegic with severe internal injuries.

Stan has caused himself incalculable grief and suffering. He will now cost the California taxpayers untold sums of money in medical expenses for the rest of his life.

What a tremendous difference between Martha the Absolved and Despondent Stan! Martha snuffed out two young lives, but is able to forgive herself for that grievous error. Stan *attempted* an illegal sexual act with a young girl, and is unable to forgive himself for his wrong.

The difference between the thinking of Martha and Stan should drive home with poignant force the importance of controlling your thought dwelling. Exercise the Force within you and you live. Do not draw upon this durable Force and you mentally die. Who is going to own *your* mind? The *choice* is yours.

It is only when we allow Satan-I in the form of the Me Dragon to get us into that obsessive, remorseful state of mind that self-condemnation sets in. "How could I be so stupid!" At this point, peace of mind is completely lost, self-detestation takes its place, and suicide sometimes follows.

We all made bad decisions. We all made stupid mistakes. We all regret (more about regret later) many things we did in our respective pasts. That is not the question. The question is how do we react to thoughts of our past errors?

Have you, my dear reader, ever committed mistakes of the same magnitude as St. Paul or Martha, namely, the killing of innocent human beings? If you have or haven't, are you able to forgive yourself for the mistakes you committed? When you think back on the most stupid thing you did, does it still really hurt? Even if you have committed supreme stupid mistakes, we can march forward and stand together to slay your Me Dragon once and for all.

Healing Steps for
Forgiving Yourself for a Past Mistake

Before we commence the Healing Steps, let us reiterate and stay focused on our goal: changing emotionally disturbing memories of some past mistake into memories that are only historical in nature, virtually void of all emotion. The most expeditious way of attaining this goal is to faithfully follow the Healing Steps. If you inexorably follow the Healing Steps, you will ravage the Me Dragon and learn to forgive yourself for your past mistakes as God commands you to do. Then you will possess enduring peace of mind. Your heart will overflow with God's contentment. God is a truly wonderful God. He is ever present to assist you in coming to peace with your past.

As you go through the Healing Steps, do not forget our rule: When, and only when you can *truthfully* affirm any given Step/statement, should you proceed to the next Step.

1. *Remember, my past does not exist.*

   I remind myself that my past does not exist except in my memory. I accept the fact that no matter how much I might wish to do so, there is nothing I can do to change a past mistake. That mistake is part of my nonexistent, immutable, and feelingless past. Since it is nonexistent, that past mistake can never again hurt me. It is only by Satan-I negative thinking that the nonexistent past mistake can continue to hurt me. Although I cannot undo the mistake, I can change the way I think about it. I shall change the way I think about my past mistakes.

2. *My mistakes are not of equal enormity.*

   One of Satan-I's greatest devices is to get me to think that all my past mistakes are of equal enormity. Obviously, that is not true. There are mistakes and there are mistakes. They are not equal in enormity. The entire process of forgiving myself for my past mistakes begins with a true assessment of the situation. If a past mistake is truly inconsequential, the moment any thought of the mistake enters my mind, I will immediately SOAP it away. I will not put up with Satan-I nonsense of dwelling on the thought of any past, inconsequential mistake. I thank God for SOAP.

3. *Determine the magnitude of my mistake.*

If objectively as possible, I determine a past mistake is serious, I must never attempt to SOAP away all thoughts of that mistake. To do so is like trying to sweep the mistake under the rug, to try to treat it as though it never happened. That would be committing a horrible mistake on top of an earlier mistake. Sometimes, Satan-I attempts to get me to do that. It would be very harmful to me. I will never do that. Instead, I promise to rely on the Healing Steps to make permanent peace with a serious past mistake.

4. *Accept the fact that I am not perfect.*

My Satan-I tries to get me into a mind set that I am infallible. I am perfect. I should never err. I am above committing stupid mistakes. If Satan-I succeeds in getting me into this mind set, she wins. Then when I think about my past errors, I think myself stupid. I hate myself. I become clay in Satan-I's hands. She molds and plays with me. Since I can control my mind set, I refuse to allow myself to be in that mind set. I am not infallible. I accept the fact that I am not perfect. I can live with that fact.

5. *I make mistakes.*

My God-I tries to get me into the proper mind set, which is that all human beings make mistakes. I am a human being. Therefore, I make mistakes. I am not perfect. I do err. I made mistakes in the past. I will make mistakes in the future. What my God-I wants me to learn is that although I make mistakes, I can deal with those mistakes and make peace with my past. I humbly accept the fact that I am fallible.

6. *Admit I was wrong.*

I candidly and with due deference admit that I was wrong. There may be some self-flagellation, "How could I have been so stupid! How could I have been so dumb! What an idiot!" But, that should not last very long. That was a dumb, stupid, or idiotic thing to do. I was wrong. I admit I was wrong. So be it.

7. *Separate me from it.*

I must not and will not be cavalier about what I did. However, I fully understand that no past mistake of mine should ever destroy my enduring peace of mind in the present moment. I must separate what I did, a stupid past mistake, from who I am, a child of God. I acknowledge that difference. "I" am not *it*; *it* is not me. I must make that separation. I promise to dwell upon who I am and not on the act I performed. My attitude must be, "Yes, I made a bad mistake in my past. But, I am not that mistake. Further, the *I* who made that mistake in the past is not who I am in the present moment. I have learned from that mistake. I have grown intellectually and spiritually. I am a much wiser person than the person who committed that stupid mistake."

8. *Ask forgiveness from anyone I wronged.*

If I have wronged another person, I admit my mistake to whomever I have wronged. I ask forgiveness. I diplomatically remind him or her that "To err is human, to forgive is divine." I pray that he or she forgive me; that would be better for both of us. However, I understand that his or her forgiveness is not a prerequisite to my forgiving myself.

9. *Make restitution.*

If monetary restitution is necessary, I make restitution to the best of my ability, or I at least make provisions for such restitution.

10. *Without God, I admit I am powerless against Satan in the form of the Me Dragon.*

I admit I am powerless against Satan in the form of the Me Dragon. It is only by drawing upon the greater Power of the Holy Spirit Who dwells within me that I am able to defeat the Me Dragon. Once I submit, I know that *I can do all things through Him Who gives me strength.* I then become invincible against my Satan-I. From this day forward, I solemnly promise to draw upon the Power of God within me to vanquish the Me Dragon. I do this by acknowledging that the Holy Spirit is at the center of my being and I humbly seek His assistance.

11. *Recognize the battle is on.*

My God-I and Satan-I are waging a never-ending battle within me. That conflict concerns my state of mind when I consider any past serious mistake. My Satan-I desires that I continue to dwell on negative thoughts about any such mistake. My God-I desires that I Obliterate such Satan-I thoughts at their inception. God wants me to only dwell upon God-I positive thoughts about the past mistake. I acknowledge that I am in the middle of this horrendous battle with Satan-I as my cunning enemy and God-I as my faithful Ally. God-I provides me with the armor and weapons to vanquish Satan-I, in the form of the Me Dragon. I promise to use this armor and these weapons to destroy the Me Dragon and make peace with my past.

12. *Obliterate the Satan-I double standard of forgiveness.*

If someone else did the same stupid thing I did, would I understand and expect that person to forgive herself? Of course I would. Then why will I not forgive myself? Why am I always harder on myself than I expect other people to be on themselves? That is the epitome of Satan-I. I now choose not to be harder on myself than I expect other people to be on themselves. From this day forward, I choose to use only one standard of forgiveness: To err is human; to forgive is divine. That is what God expects of me. When it comes to self-forgiveness, I must practice: "I shall do unto myself as I do unto others."

13. *Learn from my mistakes.*

I can learn from that mistake. In fact, some good could result from my error. I will look for the good. If in my mistake I can find good for others or myself I will do it. In the very least, if I am wise, I will not make the same mistake again. That is spiritual growth.

14. *Accept God's forgiveness.*

Even if I did murder or rape, if I seek God's forgiveness, He will forgive me. In fact, the very nanosecond I ask God to forgive me for my error, He does so. I know that with absolute certainty because He has said so. If God immediately forgives me, there is no reason for me not to forgive myself. As with St. Paul, He wants me to forgive myself and get on with His work. That is His divine command. I do forgive myself. I will get on with God's work. I will follow His divine command.

15. *Prepare for negative thoughts that prevent healing.*

My Satan-I will raise negative thoughts to prevent my healing. It is natural for that to happen. I expect it to happen. That is an attempt by my Satan-I to make me despise myself, to cause me emotional distress. Satan wants to own my mind, then my soul. Such thoughts will include:

- I never make a small mistake. All my mistakes are major stupidity.
- For now, I'll just sweep all the thoughts of the mistake under the rug. I'll come back and deal with it later.
- I can't believe I'm so stupid!
- No one else would make such a stupid mistake!

- You idiot!
- What a jerk I am!
- The person I've wronged will never forgive me. I don't blame him. I've made an enemy for life. How can I be so dumb!
- I'll never forgive myself for what I did!
- What I did was terrible.
- No one could ever love me. Why should I love myself!?
- I wish I were dead!

16. *Turn to positive healing thoughts.*

My God-I will place in my mind self-healing thoughts to assist me in making peace with my past. It is natural for that to happen. I expect it to happen. That is God-I's way of helping me to get over the effects of my past mistakes. My God-I very much desires that I have enduring peace of mind. My God-I wants me to be doing God's work, just as St. Paul did. God-I thoughts include:

- If I think about it objectively, most of my mistakes are not horrific. I must not blow my mistakes out of proportion.
- Everyone makes mistakes. I am no exception.
- I am not perfect. I never claimed to be perfect.
- To lightly dismiss this matter would be wrong. On the other hand, to not forgive myself is equally wrong.
- I am a loved child of God. I promise to dwell on who I am and not on some mistake I made. That is separating *me* from *it*.
- If my mistake involved wronging another person, I will ask that person to forgive me. For both our sakes, I hope she does so. However, her forgiving me is not a prerequisite to my forgiving myself.
- To forgive is divine. God has forgiven me. I believe that from the bottom of my heart. God *commands* me to forgive myself. I will obey God's command.

- I shall do unto myself as I would expect others to do unto themselves, i.e., forgive.
- This mistake is part of my nonexistent, immutable, and feelingless past. I accept that fact.
- If I am wise, I can grow by learning from my past mistake. I will use this mistake as a growing experience.

17. *Use* SOAP *to control my thought dwelling.*

I alone choose when to think about a past mistake. To make peace with my past, I must take control of when I do and do not think about a past mistake. I know that is extremely important. I will never just sweep thoughts of the mistake under the rug and refuse to deal with it. That is very harmful to me. On the other hand, I must dispose of Satan-I negative memories of the event swiftly and efficiently. What I promise myself is that I will never think about my mistake in terms of Satan-I negative thoughts. I promise myself I will use Stop, Obliterate, Alter, Praise every time I experience a Satan-I negative thought about the past mistake—Healing Step 15 type thoughts. I promise myself I will only dwell upon God-I healing thoughts about the mistake—Healing Step 16 type thoughts. I solemnly swear by all I hold sacred that I will never violate that rule.

18. *Stay constantly before God.*

Constantly I will say, "Please dear God, let me live only in the present and plan for the future."

19. *Repeat the Healing Steps until I am healed.*

I know I have overcome the debilitating effects of the memory of my past mistake when I can think about the mistake and it no longer has a negative emotional impact on me. The once highly emotionally disturbing memories of the mistake become nothing more than memories of an historical event virtually void of emotion. I will repeat the

Healing Steps over and over again until the memory of the past mistake becomes nothing more that the memory of an historical event. Then I am healed. Then I have made peace with my past.

In summary, the mind set that I follow to forgive myself for any past wrong is to transform emotional thoughts to historical thoughts. That is the goal. I attain that goal by repeating the Healing Steps as often as necessary.

1. Remember, my past does not exist.
2. My mistakes are not of equal enormity.
3. Determine the magnitude of my mistake.
4. Accept the fact that I am not perfect.
5. I make mistakes.
6. Admit I was wrong.
7. Separate me from it.
8. Ask forgiveness from anyone I wronged.
9. Make restitution.
10. Without God, I admit I am powerless against Satan in the form of the Me Dragon.
11. Recognize the battle is on.
12. Obliterate the Satan-I double standard of forgiveness.
13. Learn from my mistakes.
14. Accept God's forgiveness.
15. Prepare for negative thoughts that prevent healing.
16. Turn to positive healing thoughts.
17. Use SOAP to control my thought dwelling.
18. Stay constantly before God.
19. Repeat the Healing Steps until I am healed.

Regretting Past Mistakes

You say to me, "I understand that repeating the Healing Steps over and over again will generally heal me. But, honestly Mike, doesn't the Me Dragon jump up and jab you real hard now and then so that you wince when you think of that really stupid thing you did? Don't you still have significant regret for any of your past mistakes?"

I honestly tell you, "Yes, the Me Dragon does occasionally jab me really hard with a Satan-I negative thought of some stupid thing I did. And, yes, I do wince when I feel the sharp pain of my past stupidity. But I *immediately* use a shorthand cure of everything we've discussed in this chapter. When I feel the sharp pain I say three words only, 'Historical or emotional?' That puts everything into perspective for me."

Those three words are shorthand for yes, I did that stupid thing. But our loving Father forgave me. Following His command, I chose to forgive myself. I treat a mistake as a learning experience. I am different from what I did. I pray I will never repeat a mistake.

By doing that, I no longer have a fit of emotional pain when the Me Dragon thrusts upon me a thought of a nonexistent, immutable, feelingless past mistake.

"Historical or emotional?" I cannot emphasize enough how well that technique works! Every time Satan-I jabs you hard with a negative thought about that really stupid thing you did, say, "Historical or emotional?" Are you going to treat such thoughts as thoughts of a nonexistent, immutable, feelingless past historical mistake, or are you going to shout out, "How could I have been so stupid? I'm an idiot. I hate myself for being so dumb!" If the former, you are healed and "historical or emotional" works for you. If the latter, you are not yet healed and you need to repeat the Healing Steps until you are healed. I pray it is the former.

Synopsis

Say to yourself:

In a very real sense, I truly am the master of my own fate since I alone choose whether I will or will not draw upon the great Force existing within me to help me make peace with my past. Cloaked with the armor and weapons of God, I am invincible against Satan-I and his thrusting upon me negative, self-defeating thoughts of my past mistakes. By using the Healing Steps as often as necessary, memories of past dead mistakes can no longer hurt me. I can and will slay the Me Dragon every time he raises his ugly head. I revel in the Power I possess! "Where are you, Me Dragon? I beseech you, come and do battle with me!" Nothing, but peaceful silence.

GOOD LIFE TRUTHS
DERIVED FROM CHAPTER TEN

10-1. I am fallible. I made mistakes in the past. I will make mistakes in the future. Of that I am certain.

10-2. What I did, I did. It's over. It's done. It is immutable. I cannot change any past mistakes one iota. However, I realize there is no connection between any of my past mistakes and how I feel in the present moment. I realize that although I can never change any past mistake, I can change the manner in which I think about any past mistake.

10-3. What I did was stupid. However, I am not stupid. I am not any past mistake. I am not *it*. *It* is not me. I am not the same person who made that stupid mistake. I am a loved child of God. That is a distinction God never wants me to forget.

10-4. I know the nanosecond I ask God to forgive me for any past stupid mistake, it is forgiven. God then wants me to forgive myself. It is my duty to obey God's command. It is my duty to forgive myself for all my past mistakes.

10-5. I must think about all my past mistakes only in God-I positive thoughts . I must immediately SOAP away any Satan-I negative thought about a past mistake. That will allow me to slay the Me Dragon and bring me to peace with my past mistakes. I will never forget, "Historical or emotional?"

CHAPTER ELEVEN

WHAT FATE DID TO YOU IN YOUR PAST DOES NOT DETERMINE HOW YOU FEEL IN THE PRESENT MOMENT

Now it is time to face Satan in the form of the Fate Dragon who desires to destroy our enduring peace of mind by having us dwell on negative thoughts of the terrible things Fate did to us.

Fate can deal us many harmful blows: Being born with a serious handicap, experiencing a lingering illness, the untimely death of a loved one as the result of a rare disease, a devastating flood, hurricane, or fire that destroys everything we own, etc. The list is endless. How can we possibly have enduring peace of mind when one of those blows befalls us?

As always, I pray that you are sensitive to the presence of God's Divine Power at the center of your being. Without recognition of this Power, the situation would be hopeless. For people who stubbornly refuse to acknowledge His presence, the situation is often hopeless.

I further pray that with humble love, you accept the fact that your God-I is devoted to your well-being.

> I called upon Your name, O Lord, from the bottom of the pit; You heard me call, "Let not Your ear be deaf to my cry for help!" You came to my aid when I called to You; You said, "Have no fear!" You defended me in mortal danger, You redeemed my life. (Lam. 3:55–58 NAB)

I know it will not surprise you when I assert that what Fate did to you has absolutely nothing to do with how you feel in the present moment.

Accidents, Wars, Physical Illness, and Fire

It is time you met my father.

Sage Hider

My father was born near Beirut, Lebanon. His father, seeking a better life for his family, came to the United States just prior to the eruption of World War I. Little more than a boy, my father, his mother, and his younger sister were left stranded in Lebanon during the war. There was no food. Conditions were insufferable. My father and grandmother clawed through snow desperately searching for anything edible. It was all to no avail.

My aunt, eight years old at the time, died of starvation in my father's arms. My father tenderly kissed his sister good-bye and laid her emaciated body in a large pit holding innumerable innocent victims of that horrible war. There was neither time nor means to provide any type of a funeral. The long ago forgotten mass grave would have to do.

My father and my grandmother moved on. Eventually, through God's grace, they joined my grandfather in the United States.

My father began working in a glass factory, where he met my mother. Once they were married, my mother never worked outside the home. Five years after they were married, I was born, followed by three wonderful sisters.

Growing up as a lower middle class boy, there was always a paucity of money. My father and I spent thousands of hours doing home repairs and improvements, repairing cars outside in the middle of bitter-cold Ohio winters, hauling packages of compressed coal dust inside our old 1936 Hudson automobile, later building a coal bin, and then a garage. (I look back on those times as some of the most enjoyable moments of my entire life.)

Lebanese fathers and sons are especially close. That was particularly true for my father and me, since I was the only son and oldest child. However, despite our closeness and all the time we spent together, that spiritual giant never told me about his ordeal in Lebanon. There never was mention of war, digging through snow searching for grass to eat, my aunt who died in his arms, or mass graves. Quite the contrary, my father only talked about what a beautiful country Lebanon is. If our mother had not passed on the story of those war years to my sisters and me, we never would have known about that chapter of my father's life.

Let me share with you another insight about that great man: He worked at Libby Glass for forty-five years as a blue-collar worker. On one occasion, near the end of his shift, his left glove was caught in a machine and his hand slowly fed into the hungry behemoth. There was nothing he could do until the machine chewed off a substantial part of his index finger. He was rushed to the local hospital where the bone was cut back even further so skin could be grafted over the top of what remained of the finger. The next day he reported for work at the beginning of his shift as if nothing happened!

My father never filed a Workers Compensation claim or any type of lawsuit as a result of the accident. That's exactly how he viewed it, an accident!

He often included the stub of his finger as a prop in many of the jokes he was fond of telling.

My father was one of the most happy-go-lucky men I ever knew. He was the life of every family get together. He was loved by everyone. As far as I know, he never had an enemy.

Sage had two outstanding attributes: He relied on God for everything and he *never* looked back. He truly only lived in the present and planned for the future. He never wasted the precious present moment with thoughts of past traumas. He didn't have time for such nonsense.

An unknown author stated: "Mighty men shall be mightily tormented." He or she was close, but the saying is incomplete. I have taken the liberty of embellishing the statement. In the form of one of my favorite Good Life Truths, it becomes:

> Mighty men and women are mightily tormented and tenaciously arise unscathed with their enduring peace of mind intact.

That Good Life Truth well describes Sage and a few other people I hold in highest esteem. My Lebanese, immigrant father with a third grade education could not have expressed, "I alone am responsible for how I feel every conscious moment of my life," but he lived it every conscious moment of his life. And equally important, he was able to pass on that philosophy to his progeny.

Sage was keenly aware of the infinitely powerful God-I Who existed at the center of his being. He knew that Power was his for the asking. He asked. He knew the Force allowed him to eliminate Satan-I negative thinking and allowed him to be perpetually one with his God-I. Having that realization brings peace. When we finally come to that realization, we too will have peace, regardless of what Fate did to us.

Obviously, the serious illness of one's self or a loved one, a stroke, a heart attack, financial ruin, laying your sisters's rawboned corpse in a pit, or whatever Fate may send us, cannot cause us to have enduring bad feelings. Anger, sadness, and depression are *choices*. Acceptance, determination to overcome the odious feelings, to refuse to dwell on the memory of the event in Satan-I negative terms, to flush such thoughts out of our minds and to enjoy life, are also *choices*.

If you feel anger, sadness, or depression because of the hand Fate has dealt you, you are allowing Satan-I to control your mind. You are not using the God-I Force at the center of your being to SOAP away those Satan-I negative stinking-thinking thoughts. It doesn't have to be that way.

Another case in point:

Dave Roever

One of the most moving testimonials I've personally witnessed is that of Dave Roever. Dave was a United States sailor fighting in Vietnam. As part of Dave's personal arsenal, he carried white phosphorous hand grenades, the type of grenades that burn under water. During one melee, while standing on a riverbank, Dave pulled the pin on one of his grenades, drew back his arm to throw, but the grenade exploded before being thrown.

Dave was catapulted into the water, where he continued to burn. He watched forty pounds of his flesh float down-river. Most of his face was gone.

Dave was not expected to live. He was hospitalized for over a year and underwent a multitude of operations. Much of his head is plastic and parts are removable. He would be the first to tell you he is not a pretty sight.

On the other hand, he is a most beautiful man, spiritually speaking. As he says, "It has been my relationship with Him (Jesus) that has guided me through the tragedies of war, sustained me through the trauma of injury, and today continues to give direction to my life."

Dave spends most of his time visiting schools, lecturing to students, and conducting citywide crusades across the United States. His message is *From Tragedy to Triumph*, the title of one of his videotapes. He is teaching personal responsibility, waging his own war against the use of alcohol and drugs, sexual promiscuity, etc. It is a moving experience to watch him on stage. There is no way to tell how many young people he has saved from physical or emotional destruction.

Dave is the living epitome of *What Fate did to me does not determine how I feel in the present moment.* He has turned a horrible personal catastrophe into a vehicle whereby he has dramatically touched the lives of millions of young men and women. He is doing much more for God now then he could have done had Fate not intervened. Instead of being a recluse, he is wisely taking advantage of what Fate did to him to better serve God.

Like my father, Dave realizes that the most awesome Power that exists is within each of us. That Power is given to us to draw upon in our daily battle against Satan-I. It is ours for the taking. To slay Satan-I in the form of the Fate Dragon, we must recognize that Force at the center of our being. We must draw upon the Force against Satan-I. That is precisely what life is all about!

Clearly, it is not the hand Fate dealt us that determines how we feel at any given moment. It is the thought we choose to dwell upon that determines how we feel in the present moment. The Sage Hiders and Dave Roevers prove that beyond all reasonable doubt. They do not dwell upon Satan-I negative thoughts of what Fate did to them. They do not seek pity from other people, nor do they indulge in self-pity. Those type people intuitively know of and how to draw upon the Force of Almighty God within them to habitually crush every Satan-I negative thought that enters their mind. The rest of us must learn that process. When we do, we will be like those spiritual giants. Neither Sage nor Dave ever parked under that noxious cherry tree. Rather, they zoomed down the road of life mocking Satan-I's attempts to destroy their enduring peace of mind. Satan-I never had a chance with either of them.

It is this failure to recognize and draw upon the God Force at the center of our being to Obliterate Satan-I negative thoughts that differentiates the winners from the losers when it comes to battling Satan-I in the form of the Fate Dragon. My friend Jacob falls into the latter group.

Grumbling Jacob

Jacob suffers from a chronic minor ailment. It is neither life-threatening nor disabling. Jacob is required to take medication at specific times throughout the day. In addition, he has regular appointments with his doctor.

Jacob is totally consumed with his malady. It is all he talks about and apparently all he thinks about. He blames his medical problems for his perpetual mild depression. He has been under a psychiatrist's care for many years.

Jacob's usual rhetoric is, "I don't know why this happened to me. Taking this medication day in and day out is a real pain, and expensive. And doctors, doctors, doctors! No one else in my family has this problem, why me?"

The minor illness has virtually disabled Grumbling Jacob. All he thinks about is his illness, taking medication, the cost of his medication, and his doctor appointments. He has no clue that unceasingly dwelling on Satan-I negative thoughts about his health causes his feelings of discontentment. He blames his illness for his present moment feelings. He is most sadly wrong. *He has no clue that by controlling his thought dwelling, he could completely change his life.*

Through unjustifiable ignorance, Jacob and many people like him, cause their own discontentment. Unknowingly, many people withhold peace of mind from themselves. The message that they are the temples of the Holy Spirit, that the Power of God resides within them, that they can be the masters of their thought dwelling, has fallen on deaf ears. That is unfortunate. Jacob envisions himself as a victim. Clearly, he is a chronic victim. But it is of his own making. You know very well where he is parked. *Plop. Plop. Plop.*

When we acknowledge, accept, and draw upon God-I and His unlimited Power, we can overcome Satan-I *every* moment of our lives. Then we have a conscious and splendid realization of wholeness, of being one with God, of peace. When we are in that state of mind, it is as if Satan-I does not exist. The Sages and Roevers of the world are of that state of mind. They live at a higher level of consciousness than most people. They are our models.

So is my friend, Tony.

Titan Tony

As the result of a series of strokes, Tony is paralyzed from the neck down. He has great difficulty speaking. He never really talks.

Tony is confined to a wheelchair or laying flat on his back twenty-four hours a day. His family cares for him day and night. It is unlikely his condition will ever dramatically improve.

When I visit Tony, there is much camaraderie. When I tell him the latest joke I've heard, he almost rolls off the couch in uncontrollable laughter. Despite his physical condition, he has maintained a great disposition and sense of humor.

During one of my visits, his son was sitting on the back of the couch where Titan Tony was laying. He said, "Dad, I don't want to get too close to you because of my laryngitis." Tony responded, tortuously pronouncing or spelling one word at a time, "Yes, I don't want to get laryngitis because I won't be able to speak." Once we understood the sentence and repeated it back to him, he laughed wildly.

It is a blessing to be in the presence of Tony and his family. They are living examples of two important Good Life Truths:

What Fate did to me does not determine how I feel in the present moment.

I alone am responsible for how I feel every conscious moment of my life, regardless of what Fate did to me.

Fate dealt Tony and his family a hard blow, but without crippling mental injury. They are wise.

What causes the difference between Grumbling Jacob's state of mind and Titan Tony's state of mind? I think you know. Controlling your thought dwelling is everything when it comes to possessing enduring peace of mind.

One of my favorite stories dealing with being in control of your thought dwelling and resulting feelings when the Fate Dragon besets you with a traumatic event, is about Thomas Edison:

Thomas Edison

In 1914, Thomas Edison's factory in New Jersey was destroyed by fire. Much of Edison's life's work went up in flames and smoke. At the height of the fire, Edison shouted to his son, "Charles, bring your mother. She will never again see anything like this."

The next morning, Edison looked at the ruins and stated, "There is great value in disaster. All our mistakes are burned up. Thank God we can start anew." Three weeks later, Edison delivered his first phonograph.

A less understanding man would have been devastated by such a disaster. However, that great genius certainly understood that Fate delivers traumatic blows to each of us throughout our lives on earth. He also understood that unless we allow it, those Fate events do not control how we feel in the present moment. If Edison's actions don't drive home the point I'm trying to make, then I fear that nothing I can say will ever convince you that:

> I alone am responsible for how I feel every conscious moment of my life, regardless of what Fate did to me.

Each of us gives meaning to any Fate-event that comes into our lives. The wise, acknowledging and utilizing the Power of God within them, expeditiously get Satan-I negative stinking-thinking of the traumatic event behind them, and magnificently get on with their lives. Those are the Sages, Roevers, Tonys, and Edisons of the world.

Then there are those people who by ignorance, or by willfully turning their backs on God, have no idea of what to do when Fate deals them a hard blow. They view themselves as chronic victims. They each sit under their mental cherry tree, foot pressed hard against the brake pedal, with that awesome Power going to waste. *Plop. Plop. Plop.*

God begs us to draw upon the Power He infused in us to constantly rid ourselves of Satan-I negative thoughts and only dwell upon God-I positive thoughts about what Fate did to us. That is the relationship with God to which we must all aspire. That is precisely what Jesus did. That is precisely what we must do. We must do that no matter what Fate did to us.

Gender, Race, Color, Physical Attributes, and Handicaps

Fate, in the form of physical laws, gives us gender, race, color, physical attributes, and handicaps. However, just as past trauma does not determine our feelings in the present moment, neither does gender, race, color, physical attributes and handicaps determine our present moment feelings.

We can use any of those things as lame excuses for why we feel so badly. We can say people are prejudiced against us because of our gender, race, color, appearance, age, and handicaps, and therefore we are immobilized. Or, we can push ahead using as models those minorities, disabled, and far less than perfect persons who excelled in every major endeavor of the human race.

Who has not heard of the blind, deaf, but charismatic Helen Keller? Even though he was a cripple, Franklin Delano Roosevelt was elected President of the United States for an unprecedented four consecutive terms.

Many accomplished entertainers are much less than handsome or beautiful. Jimmy Durante, the "Schnoz," became a famous movie star despite and partially because of his very large nose. Think what the world would have lost if Ray Charles or Stevie Wonder had let the fact that they were Black and blind keep them from daring to become showmen. Sammy Davis Jr. used to joke about the fact that he was a Black Jew with only one eye. Obviously he did not let it prevent him from becoming one of the greatest and most wealthy entertainers of his time.

Every career field has its "disadvantaged" persons. I know a judge and a very victorious football coach, neither of whom have hands. How many successful handicapped persons do you know?

Fate, in one form or another, has dealt each of those persons a blow. But, it was a blow without injury. They each realized what Fate did to them has absolutely nothing to do with how they feel in the present moment. They accepted the challenge and viciously killed every negative thought Satan-I threw at them. Each undauntedly moved forward with his or her life. Each faced his or her Fate Dragon and slew it.

It is clearly our choice.

Upbringing

Another mask the Fate Dragon wears is the circumstance of our upbringing. Many people complain about their upbringing. Foolishly, they *blame* their upbringing for their present moment discontentment. Some of those people were raised poor, in the ghetto, many miles from another family, etc. Of course, that has absolutely nothing to do with our present moment feelings. Donna is living proof of that fact.

Intrepid Donna

Many years ago when I was in engineering, Donna was one of my co-workers. She was happily married, a good mother, very professional, proficient, neat in appearance, and always pleasant.

I assumed Donna was raised in a typical middle class family. (Being a judge for fifteen years, I am *slowly* learning to not make very many assumptions.) One day, almost in passing, I inquired about her upbringing. I was so overwhelmed with her story I requested that she write it out for me. What follows is a condensed version:

> I was born and spent the first years of my life in (a small agricultural town). I was an only child.
> I was one of the top students in my early elementary school years. I very much enjoyed this time in school.

My parents were always kind to me. However, I now realize they were mildly retarded. Of course at the time, I had no way of knowing this. Considering their mental condition, they did the best they could for us.

When I was eight years of age, we moved into a dilapidated house in a remote part of the county. More correctly, it was a shack with no electricity, gas, or water. It was not pleasant.

My parents and I did farm work and odd jobs year round. I was taken out of school. I had no opportunity to socialize with any children my own age. I did not return to school for almost four years.

Someone, maybe an angel, anonymously reported our situation to Child Protective Services. They came to our house and conducted an investigation. They found substandard housing with many broken windows. The house was filthy. The back door was completely missing. One room was not being used due to a fire that had occurred prior to our moving into the house. The debris from the fire had never been removed. We had foam mats on the floor with soiled sleeping bags for beds. There was a bucket in the corner containing urine and feces. There was a dead rat in front of the camp stove.

I was removed from my parents' custody and placed in a foster home. I returned to school. At first, it was very difficult for me to fit in with other children. But, by God's grace, I did eventually acclimate. By the time I graduated, I was in the top one-third of my class.

I have maintained a good relationship with my parents. As I said, they did the best they could.

Mike, I heard you say many times, "I alone am responsible for how I feel every conscious moment of my life." Somehow, I always knew this.

Concerning upbringing, Donna said it all. There is nothing I can add.

However, there is so much exciting evidence that we possess the Power to slay Satan in the form of the Fate Dragon that I am compelled to share yet another uplifting anecdote with you. Dave Thomas, the founder of Wendy's International, is another hero of mine.

Dave Thomas

Dave was born in 1932 during the Great Depression. He was born in New Jersey to a woman out of wedlock. He never knew his biological father or mother. Just after his birth, he was adopted and moved to Michigan. Unfortunately, his adoptive mother died when he was five years old.

Continuing from Dave's book, *Well Done!*:

Although I was lucky that my adoptive father kept me with him, most of my younger years were spent in trailers and modest apartments as he moved around tracking down work and going through two other marriages. It wasn't an easy life by any means, but I survived.

I started working in the restaurant business full-time when I was only twelve, at the Regas Restaurant in Knoxville, Tennessee. The owners of the restaurant where I worked, Frank and George Regas, were my first mentors. I adopted Frank, George, and their workers as my family. Even though at first they didn't know how young I was, they took me under their wing and taught me a very important lesson: *as long as you try, you can be anything you want to be . . .*

When my family moved to Fort Wayne, Indiana, so that my adoptive dad could find work, I got a job at the Hobby House Restaurant working for Phil Clauss. Phil was another important mentor, and I felt adopted by his workers. Because I worked long hours, *I dropped out of high school when I was fifteen. That was a big mistake, but by then I had left my family and was living at the YMCA.*

At eighteen I enlisted in the army and was lucky enough to become a sergeant who worked at an Enlisted Man's Club while I was stationed in Germany. When I got out of the service, I went back to the Hobby House. . . .

About that time, I also got to know Colonel Harland Sanders pretty well. The Colonel was franchising his Kentucky Fried Chicken idea to restaurants that were already up and running at that time—selling his pressure cookers and his blend of spices and herbs out of the back of his car.

In 1962 I got the chance to move to Columbus, Ohio, to see if I could turn around four failing Kentucky Fried Chicken restaurants. The Colonel and others told me I was dumb to try, but I did it anyway. It worked. I became an on-paper millionaire as a result and then sold out my interest, becoming rich enough (and whacko enough) to build a swimming pool in our backyard in the shape of a chicken.

There's no reason in the world that a dirt-poor kid like me with a jumbled home life who dropped out of school should have made it, but I did—at least in some ways. And if I can, you can. Anybody can.

Success starts inside. Unless your own attitude and beliefs are right, you can never be a success in the world around you. (Emphasis added).

In the final analysis, it really doesn't matter what hand Fate dealt you, does it?

Death of a Loved One

One of the Fate Dragon's most horrifying scourges may be the death of a loved one, especially a child.

Judy the Endurer

Judy and her sixteen-year-old daughter, Martha, had taken separate cars to an evening church service because of errands each attended to before the service. After the service, Martha departed just ahead of Judy. They lived in the country, about ten miles from Merced.

As they neared home, Judy was driving directly behind her daughter. They were traveling the legal speed limit of fifty-five miles per hour.

Because of a catastrophic mechanical failure, Martha's car suddenly swerved to the right, struck a large oak tree, and burst into flames. Judy attempted to get to her daughter's car, but the heat was too intense. She could hear Martha screaming. Then the screaming stopped.

The next few years were very difficult for Judy. She continually mourned the loss of Martha. They were very close. Judy spent much time alone.

Fortunately, Judy enlisted the services of a very good psychotherapist. She put Judy on a regular work and social schedule. She also got Judy heavily involved in volunteer work.

Eventually, Judy was able to triumphantly slay the Fate Dragon when Satan-I bombarded her mind with thoughts of Martha's tragic death. She pulled away from the cherry tree. Judy is very active in her church, the community at large and especially in her political party where she is a dynamic force. It is a pleasure being in her company.

Let us consider another anecdote about a true hero.

Seng the Survivor

Merced County is blessed with a large intra-cultural population of Blacks, Caucasians, Mexican-Americans, etc. At the present time, no single race comprises a majority of the county's population.

One invigorating subculture is people from Southeast Asia, especially Laos. Laos is a country sandwiched between Thailand and Vietnam. The Hmong community is one of the largest of the Laotian groups. I love their hot and spicy food, of which my friend "Momma" keeps me in good supply. It is a great pleasure knowing these people.

But conditions were often deplorable in their own country during the Vietnam War. Seng is a living example of the wretched conditions some of these people were subjected to and endured.

Seng was born in Laos. He was a young boy during the Vietnam War. His family was dedicated to assisting the United States Forces during that infamous war. Early in the war, Seng's father paid with his life while rendering such assistance. However, the family continued to aid the Americans.

On one vile day, the Communists overran Seng's village. All of the strong young men were pulled aside to be used by the invaders as pack animals. The assailants then had their way with the women of the village. Seng witnessed three of his sisters brutally raped. He bolted to intervene in the atrocity but was knocked unconscious by a vicious blow from a soldier's rifle.

Thereafter, except for the young men who were separated, the villagers were lined up and machined gunned to death. That included Seng's mother, his three sisters and three little brothers.

He regained consciousness as the bloodshed ended.

At the end of the war, Seng and many of his fellow villagers made their way to Merced County. A good number of them are business owners, professionals, and community leaders. Seng is both a business owner and a community leader. He is very positive, outgoing, and a tremendous asset to our community.

I have enjoyed many long discussions with Judy the Endurer and Seng the Survivor concerning the untimely and violent deaths of their family members. It is a pleasure talking and sharing ideas with them. They are indeed mighty warriors.

Judy and Seng slew their respective Fate Dragons. It took time, but they won. We can learn much from these wonderful people.

If the Fate Dragon dealt you one of these ghastly blows, and you have lost a loved one, or an entire family, how can you regain your enduring peace of mind?

I can speak with some confidence since both of my parents, with whom I was very close and very much loved, are dead.

In my discussions with Judy and Seng, we agreed that the most expeditious manner of dealing with the thoughts of the death of a loved one is to consider the totality of the circumstances. We must first consider the very real loss to us of a dearly beloved. Then, for our own well-being, it is imperative that we consider death from the departed person's point of view.

From Our Point of View

We must ask, when we grieve for a deceased loved one, are we really grieving for him or her, or for ourselves? Clearly, we are grieving for ourselves. As long as it is not excessive, to the point of destroying our enduring peace of mind, it is natural and healthy to do so. If it is excessive, it is the Fate Dragon viciously attacking us, attempting to consume and devour us, depriving us of present moment enduring peace of mind. We cannot let this occur.

My parents have been dead for many years. I still very much miss them, but not to the point of destroying my enduring peace of mind.

I particularly enjoyed the long telephone conversations with my parents. My mother was the family historian. It was always a delightful experience being brought current with the happenings in the lives of my aunts, uncles, siblings, nieces, nephews, and friends. We could talk for hours.

My parents truly enjoyed California. I looked forward with great expectation to their visits from Ohio. We thrilled at travelling through Northern California, camping in magnificent Yosemite National Park, Napa Valley with its wonderful wineries, driving along the Mendicino Coast, the incredible beauty of Mt. Shasta, and many wonderful weekends spent in tantalizing San Francisco, probably the most beautiful city in the world.

But, Southern California also delighted us. The breathtaking drive along Highway 1, the wonderful California Missions stretching along hundreds of miles of coastline, inimitable Hearst Castle, and the excitement of Disneyland where we could once again be children.

I very much miss the phone calls. I very much miss the visits. I wish they had never ended. But they did. For this, I am sad.

Anyone who has lost a dearly beloved shares these emotions.

From the Decedent's Point of View

Any departed beloved is now enjoying the fulfillment of the blessed hope, resting in God's bosom, while we are still in this vale of tears. What truly religious person would not immediately choose the former over the latter? Eternal ecstasy and bliss versus daily conflicts with Satan-I is an easy choice.

Judy and Seng made another indisputable point: How would our departed loved one want us to act? Would that departed Soul want us to unceasingly grieve, continually losing the peace of the present moment? We think not. That dear person would want us to get on with our lives, to stop grieving, which is more for ourselves than the deceased person. Our deceased beloved would beg us to let go and get on with living and doing God's work.

I recently attended a friend's funeral. His family chose this epitaph for his Memorial Card:

<u>Miss Me—But Let Me Go</u>

When I come to the end of the road
   And the sun has set for me
I want no rites in a gloom filled room-
   Why cry for a Soul set free?

Miss me a little—but not too long
   And not with your head bowed low
Remember the love that we once shared
   Miss me—but let me go.

For this journey that we all must take
   And each must go alone
It's all a part of the Master's plan
   A step on the road to home.

When you are lonely or sick of heart
   Go to the friends we know
And bury your sorrows in doing good deeds
   Miss me—but let me go.

—Author unknown

When we view death from the departed person's point of view, death is not sad and it has no sting. As always, the Bible is so correct:

Where, O death, is your victory? Where, O death, is your sting? (I Corinthians 15:55 NIV).

God led Judy, Seng, and me to an important realization. If we were granted the awesome power to recall any departed loved one back from heaven to earth, would we exercise that power? We all unhesitatingly agreed that we would never exercise that option. If you possessed that incredicble power, would you call a dearly beloved back from heaven? I suspect not. If I am correct, do you now realize the foolishness and demonic source of our excessively grieving for the loss of a loved one who is in the Golden City?

Excessive grieving does absolutely nothing for the departed person. But, it can cause us serious harm. Excessive grieving is a vicious Fate Dragon that must be slain.

Do I miss the long talks and wonderful visits with my parents? Words cannot describe how very much I miss that interaction!

If granted the power, would I summon them back from Paradise? *Never!*

In this chapter, we experienced the Fate Dragon in many forms. We discussed accidents, wars, physical illnesses, fire, race, color, physical attributes, handicaps, upbringing, and the death of a loved one. Obviously, the Fate Dragon can take on many other forms, e.g., floods, hurricanes, earthquakes, mental retardation, AIDS, etc. The list is endless. But so is the list of heroes who confronted the Fate Dragon in each of those situations and slew him.

By following the Healing Steps, we can be equally victorious against the Fate Dragon, regardless of what obstacles he has thrown across our path of life.

Healing Steps to Overcome What Fate Did to You

As you proceed through the Healing Steps, please remember: Only when you can *truthfully* affirm any given Step/statement, should you proceed to the next Step.

Repeat this process as often as you need it.

With courage and love in your heart, and acknowledging God at the center of your being, proceed.

1. *Fate's blows are inescapable.*

    I realize trauma caused by Fate flows into everyone's life. There are absolutely no exceptions. I am no exception. It is part of the human experience. I accept the fact that I am not singled out for Fate's blows. I am ready to no longer feel, "Why me! Oh, poor me!"

2. *I shall overcome.*

    If, when I think about what Fate did to me, I become angry, sad, or depressed, then I realize I have given my mind over to the Fate Dragon. That is very harmful to me. I am hurting myself. I do not want to hurt myself. I do not want to be consumed with anger, sadness, or depression. I want to heal myself of those Satan-I negative feelings. It is absolutely essential to my mental and physical well-being that I overcome the Satan-I negative thoughts that are causing those negative feelings of anger, sadness, or depression. I shall heal myself of these Satan-I negative thoughts. With the God-Force within me, I can muster the self-discipline to do so. I shall do so. I shall overcome the Fate Dragon.

3. *Without God, I admit I am powerless against Satan in the form of the Fate Dragon.*

    I admit I am powerless against Satan in the form of the Fate Dragon. It is only by submitting to the greater Power of the Holy Spirit Who dwells within me that I am able to defeat the Fate Dragon. Once I submit, I know that *I can do all things through Him Who gives me strength.* I then become invincible against my Satan-I. From this day forward, I solemnly promise to draw upon the Power of God within me to vanquish the Fate Dragon.

4. *God is here to help me.*

    Anger, sadness, and depression are completely personal things. My anger is my anger. My sadness is my sadness. My depression is my depression. They don't belong to anyone else. I own them. Unfortunately, it is like owning rotten garbage. I do not want to own rotten garbage. I do not want to own anger, sadness, or depression. I choose to put those things with my rotten garbage, in the garbage can. God has told me He will pick up my garbage of anger, sadness, and depression. Therefore, I let God forever carry away my anger, sadness, and depression resulting from my negative thoughts of what Fate did to me.

5. *Stop blaming Fate.*
    I truly desire to be healed from the heinous thoughts of what Fate did to me. To be healed means that, despite what Fate did to me, I must take full responsibility for how I feel in the present moment. I can no longer *blame* Fate for how I feel in the present moment. I accept total responsibility for my present moment feelings. I will never again *blame* what Fate did to me for how I feel in the present moment.

6. *I accept that I cannot change what Fate did to me.*
    What Fate did to me, Fate did to me. It's over. It's done. It's ancient history. I accept it as immutable. The Fate Dragon will attempt to trap me into dwelling on Satan-I negative thoughts of what Fate did to me. I will not succumb to such chicanery. I can accept what Fate sent me. I do accept what Fate did to me. It is time to move on. I shall move on.

7. *There is hope.*
    I know what Fate did to me wasn't good. In fact, it was very bad. However, I also consider what Fate did to other people. People who had brothers or sisters die of starvation in their arms. People blown apart by a phosphorus hand grenade, suffering a series of major crippling strokes, losing everything they've worked for in a fire or flood, being raised in a remote hovel, or the untimely snuffing out of the life of a loved one. Yet, those people all overcame what Fate did to them. That gives me great hope. I gain strength

from the strength of others. If they are able to slay the Fate Dragon, so can I! I am determined to do so! I shall do so!

8. *The need to control my thought dwelling.*

I will never attempt to sweep under the rug *every* thought of what Fate did to me and attempt never to think about it. Such an attempt would be futile and very harmful to me. I know I must bravely face and asassinate the Fate Dragon. I know I must never think about what Fate did to me in terms of Satan-I negative thoughts, but only in terms of God-I positive thoughts. I can do that. I shall face and destroy the Fate Dragon!

9. *Prepare for negative thoughts that prevent healing.*

My Satan-I will inundate my mind with negative thoughts to prevent my healing. That is characteristic of Satan-I. It is natural. I expect it to happen. Such thoughts will include:

- Why was I born this race?
- Why was I born this color?
- Why was I born with this ugly physical attribute?
- Why was I born with this handicap?
- Why did I have this kind of an upbringing?
- Why did this terrible thing happen to me?
- I loved her so much,why did she have to die so young?
- How is it I got cancer?
- Everything I owned went up in smoke!
- I'll never get over this!
- It's hopeless.
- Oh, poor me!
- Anyone, please pity me!

10. *God-I thoughts that lead to healing.*

My God-I will raise self-enriching, self-healing thoughts to assist me in my healing. That is characteristic of God-I.

It is natural for that to happen. I expect it to happen. It is an effort by my God-I to prevent me from dwelling on negative thoughts of what Fate did to me. My God-I very much desires that I have enduring peace of mind. Such God-I thoughts include:

- There are many people of my color who are successful. I can be one of them.
- There are many people of my race who are successful. I can be one of them.
- There are many people with terrible physical attributes who are successful. I can be one of them.
- There are many people with horrendous handicaps who are successful. I can be one of them.
- I still naively expect life on this earth to be perfect. It is not. I'm going to stop being so naive.
- I haven't been singled out to be hurt by Fate's blows. It happens to everyone. It is part of the human experience.
- What Fate did to me could have been a lot worse. In a sense, I'm blessed that nothing more happened to me. Thank God it wasn't worse.
- What Fate did to me wasn't really that bad. When I start feeling sorry for myself, I promise to compare what Fate did to me to with the horrible things Fate did to other people. I never experienced starvation, explosions, a series of strokes, fires, floods, abject poverty, witnessing the fiery death of a loved one, or the annihilation of my entire family. People overcome those Fate experiences and now enjoy enduring peace of mind. That is a source of great hope for me. If other people overcome such horrible Fate experiences, so can I.
- I know I have the magnificent Power of God at the center of my being. By calling upon this Power I can overcome negative thoughts about what Fate did to me. I

shall constantly draw upon the Power of God dwelling within me! I shall slay the Fate Dragon.

- I promise myself that I will only dwell upon the above type of God-I positive thoughts in working through my healing of what Fate did to me.

11. *Following God's plan.*

I alone choose what thoughts to dwell upon about what Fate did to me. In working through my healing, I must take complete and absolute control of when I do and do not think about what Fate did to me. I know this is extremely important. I choose to SOAP away the negative thoughts of what Fate did to me for a very selfish reason, so that I can possess enduring peace of mind. That is God's plan. I shall follow God's plan.

12. *Use the awesome power of SOAP!*

What I promise myself is that I will never think about what Fate did to me in terms of Satan-I negative thoughts. I promise myself I will habitually and immediately use Stop, Obliterate, Alter, Praise *every time* I experience a Satan-I negative thought about what Fate did to me— Healing Step 9 type thoughts. There will never be an exception. To work through my healing, I promise myself I will only dwell upon God-I healing thoughts about what Fate did to me—Healing Step 10 type thoughts. I solemnly swear by all I hold sacred that I will never violate that rule. I now take full responsibility for my ill feelings resulting from my continuing to dwell upon such Satan-I negative thoughts. I will never again dwell upon such thoughts. Thank God for SOAP!

13. *Knowing When I Have Vanquished The Fate Dragon.*

I know I have overcome the crippling effects of what Fate did to me when I can think about the matter and it no longer has a debilitating emotional impact on me. The once highly emotionally disturbing thoughts of the incident become nothing more than memories of an historical event virtually void of emotion. Then I am healed. I will repeat the Healing Steps over and over again until the thought of what Fate did to me becomes nothing more than thoughts of an historical event.

14. *It really doesn't matter what Fate did to me!*
      I now firmly believe that no matter what Fate did to me, it really doesn't matter. Not even my Satan-I can destroy my enduring peace of mind because of what Fate did to me, *unless I allow it*. I choose not to allow it.

In summary:

1. Fate's blows are inescapable.
2. I shall overcome.
3. Without God, I admit I am powerless against Satan in the form of the Fate Dragon.
4. God is here to help me.
5. Stop blaming Fate.
6. I accept that I cannot change what Fate did to me.
7. There is hope.
8. The need to control my thought dwelling.
9. Prepare for negative thoughts that prevent healing.
10. God-I thoughts that lead to healing.
11. Following God's plan.
12. Use the awesome power of SOAP!
13. Knowing when I have vanquished the Fate Dragon
14. It really doesn't matter what Fate did to me!

There you have it. You can become a Sage, Roever, Tony, Edison, Donna, Dave Thomas, Judy, or Seng. It is your choice. No matter what Fate did to you, it really doesn't matter. You will soon be saying and meaning:

Nice try Satan in the form of the Fate Dragon! But, what you did to me no longer has an emotional impact on me. You no longer have any control over me. I have arrived at a point of spiritual growth wherein I seldom think about what you did to me. When you shoot into my mind a negative thought about what you did to me, I unemotionally SOAP it away. It doesn't hurt anymore.

I have a life to lead. I choose to live only in the present, the here and now, and to plan for the future. I have defeated you. I am the victor. I have killed you, the Fate Dragon. Farewell forever you Satan-I negative feelings.

May you fully feel the peace of God, which you already possess, at the center of your being.

Synopsis

Say to yourself:

Today, I put on the armor of God. I drew upon the God given awesome Power within me to rid myself of any and all emotional baggage which I have been carrying as a result of the hand Fate dealt me. I know what Fate did to me has absolutely nothing to do with how I feel in the present moment. I control my feelings by controlling my thought dwelling. I Obliterate every Satan-I negative thought of what Fate did to me. I no longer blame Fate for my present moment feelings. I confronted my Fate Dragon and slew him. The Fate Dragon lies dead at my feet. I choose enduring peace of mind. I choose to complete my good life puzzle. I choose to live only in the present, the here and now, and plan for the future. I revel in those choices. Never again will I make the horrible mistake of letting what Fate did to me in one of my yesterdays destroy the peace of my today. I choose to be forever free of the Fate Dragon.

Good Life Truths
Derived from Chapter Eleven

11-1. What Fate did to me does not determine how I feel in the present moment.

11-2. I alone am responsible for how I feel every conscious moment of my life, regardless of what Fate did to me.

11-3. If other people can recover from their Fate traumas, it irrefutably proves to me that I, too, can recover from the trauma of what Fate did to me, if I truly want to.

11-4. I use Stop, Obliterate, Alter, Praise when I am experiencing Satan-I negative thoughts about the hand Fate dealt me. I deliberately choose only to dwell upon God-I positive thoughts when I think about the hand that Fate dealt me. By doing that, I viciously slay the Fate Dragon.

11-5. Mighty men and women are mightily tormented and tenaciously arise unscathed with their enduring peace of mind intact.

Epilogue

Well, my dear friend, we journeyed a long distance together. It's been a very good journey. When you first picked up this book, you held some of God's precious ideas in your hands. Now you hold them in your mind and heart.

We began our journey knowing nothing about the damaging misconceptions of a nonexistent, immutable, feelingless past; nothing about God-I, Satan-I, the Good Life Truths, Healing Steps, SOAP, nor Satan's three fire-breathing Dragons. But we learned together. I learned much in writing this book for you. I trust you learned much in reading these thoughts, for which I take no credit.

Now we clearly understand what our God meant when He said *"Peace I leave with you; my peace I give to you. Not as the world gives do I give it to you. Do not let your hearts be troubled or afraid."*

We met some wonderful people during our travels. We are deeply indebted to Luminary Mary, Wise David, Victor Frankl, Dave Roever, Adeline Hider, Titan Tony, Thomas Edison, Sage Hider, Absolved Martha, Sam Huddleston, St. Paul, and many others who gave us rest, nourishment, and encouragement along the way. Those wise people showed us how to weave a path safely through the labyrinth of life.

You donned the splendid armor of Good Life Truths and Healing Steps. You took up the mighty and shiny sword of SOAP. You fearlessly faced the Other People Dragon and slew her. You courageously confronted the Me Dragon and slew him. Then you unflinching opposed the seething Fate Dragon and slew her. They lay at your feet, utterly destroyed. They can never again hurt you. You did well. You won.

Should those despicable beasts attempt to reappear in your life, like a Phoenix, you will victoriously slay them again, and again, and again. Because of your Divine armor, your shiny sword, and the Force of Almighty God within you, you are now invincible. Concerning your past, it is as if Satan-I never existed.

Contemplate what you did. Any emotional baggage from your past no longer weighs you down. The heavy load is forever gone. Nothing from your past can ever again hurt you or take away the peace of your today. You made permanent peace with your past. This is truly a glorious day.

You toiled long and hard to develop the proper mind habits. You attained your lofty goal. You richly deserve a respite. Sheath your sword. Lay aside your armor and trusty sword. But lay them not too far away. And never, never lay away the God-Force Who dwells at the center of your being.

Now, you think in new dimensions. Unburdened by your past, you are at a much higher level of consciousness. You are truly and completely in the present moment only. Instead of wasting much energy on carrying emotional baggage, you can concentrate all your energy on enjoying the present, the amazing here and now. With great blessedness and peace in your heart you are able to say:

> I am now poised on the shore of the sea of great peace and contentment. I realize how ephemeral are all Satan-I negative thoughts of my nonexistent, immutable, feelingless past. Through the Infinite Force, I am able to cast all *future* negative

thoughts of my past life into this sea. There is much more to living than dwelling upon Satan-I negative thoughts of my past. There is love, power, happiness, peace, and *freedom*.

I am ready for a lifetime of enduring peace of mind. This is the exciting opportunity to be forever united with my awesome God-I. This is *complete* freedom from my past. I have transcended my past! I can fly with God-I! I can go higher. I can truly be *alive* with no emotional baggage to weigh me down. I now clearly understand what I intuitively knew all my life: I will never again allow what happened in one of my nonexistent, immutable, feelingless yesterdays to destroy the peace of my present moment. At last, I am free and at peace.

My being is now in rare air. I actually *feel* the realization that I live at a higher level of consciousness than I ever before lived. I cohabit with the wise. I am wise.

I see there is really only the present. There is no past. There is only here and now. I will always remain in the here and now.

I see there is only peace. It is a quiet calm peace. Unless I allow it, nothing or no one can ever again hurt me. I will not allow it. I will never again hurt myself with Satan-I negative thinking about my past.

Since I alone control my thought dwelling, then I alone am responsible for how I feel every conscious moment of my life. I exult in this control. I rejoice in this responsibility.

I am one with God-I. I can faintly glimpse Heaven. I see God more clearly. God is good. God is very good. God is love. I love God more than I ever before loved Him. Because of that love, I love myself. I also love all my neighbors.

I understand that the God-Force within me gives me enduring peace of mind. I have enduring peace. I am enduring peace.

Until I have the honor and pleasure of meeting and conversing with you in Heaven, the joyful eternal Here and Now where there is no Satan-I, may our wonderful God, the true Force, richly bless you my dearly beloved.

APPENDIX

SUMMARY OF
GOOD LIFE TRUTHS

CHAPTER ONE
Parked Under the Cherry Tree

1-1. The most valuable thing I can own is enduring peace of mind, a feeling of total contentment, of God's perpetual peace at the center of my being.

1-2. I can never possess enduring peace of mind until I make peace with my past.

1-3. A divine and awesome Power lives within me. I must learn how to draw upon this incredible Power to make peace with my past.

1-4. I must never let the thoughts of what happened in one of my yesterdays destroy the peace of my today.

1-5. I know I have overcome the crippling effects of the memory of a past event when I can think about that event and it no longer has a debilitating emotional impact on me. The once highly disturbing memories of that event become nothing more than memories of an historical event, virtually void of emotion. When I attain that state of mind, I am healed.

CHAPTER TWO
Mary, Pamela, and the Rest of Us

2-1.   Past events, in and of themselves, cannot cause me to feel unhappy in the present moment. That is because once an event is over it can no longer hurt me.

2-2.   It is negative thinking about past events that hurts me. That is a difference I must never forget. Past events cannot hurt me. Only my negative thinking about past events can hurt me.

2-3.   The type of thought I choose to dwell upon determines how I feel at any conscious moment of my life.

2-4.   I alone am responsible for how I feel every conscious moment of my life.

2-5.   I am the only person who can prevent me from possessing enduring peace of mind. No other person can take enduring peace of mind away from me. Nobody can, just me.

2-6.   The correct habits of mind give me enduring peace of mind. With the correct habits of mind, life may send me challenges, but it can never destroy my enduring peace of mind.

CHAPTER THREE
Taking Control of Your Thought Dwelling

3-1.   Whether I like it or not, God and Satan have been part of my being since the moment of my conception.

3-2.   My God-I sends a continuous flow of positive, self-enriching thoughts into my mind. My Satan-I sends a continuous flow of negative, self-defeating thoughts into my mind.

3-3.   I alone choose how long I dwell upon any thought which enters my mind.

3-4.   There is nothing which affects my well-being more than controlling the type of thought upon which I dwell.

3-5.   The key to making peace with my past is to control the type of thoughts upon which I dwell.

CHAPTER FOUR
STOP, OBLITERATE, Alter, Praise (SOAP)

4-1.   I have absolutely no control over past events. They are dead and gone forever. However, I have absolute control over how long I dwell upon negative thoughts about past events and the negative feelings that flow therefrom.

4-2.   Without exception, negative thought dwelling always precedes negative feelings. If I eliminate my negative thought dwelling, I eliminate my negative feelings.

4-3.   Being wise means persistently exercising self-discipline to draw upon the God Power Who dwells within me to perpetually control my thought dwelling.

4-4.   Stop, Obliterate, Alter, Praise, is the only methodology that gives me complete control of my thought dwelling.

4-5.   To make peace with my past, I must *habitually* SOAP away Satan-I negative thinking about my past. There can never be an exception to this rule. Never!

CHAPTER FIVE
The Past Does Not Exist

5-1. The events that occurred in my past are gone forever. All that remains in the present moment are my memories of nonexistent past events. Therefore, my past does not exist, except in my memory.

5-2. Since my memory alone holds my past, and I can deal with my memory, then I can deal with my past.

5-3. Events from my past cannot hurt me. Only Satan-I negative stinking-thinking about a past event can hurt me. Knowing that, I will habitually and vigorously SOAP away every Satan-I negative thought about a past event.

5-4. I must never attempt to Obliterate *all* thoughts of a non-existent past event. If I do so, I will never make peace with my past.

5-5. Correctly thinking about nonexistent past events can be very valuable to me and can lead to gainful insight about myself.

CHAPTER SIX
One's Past Can Never Be Changed

6-1. No matter how rich, powerful, or famous I am, I cannot change by one splinter an event from my past. What has happened, has happened. What was, was, and will be forever more. It's over. It's done forever.

6-2. I must unequivocally accept the fact that every past event in my life is unchangeable.

6-3. I realize it is not unchangeable past events that cause me discontentment. It is choosing to dwell upon Satan-I negative thoughts about unchangeable past events that causes me discontentment.

6-4.   I must never again dwell upon Satan-I self-defeating thoughts of wishing I could change anything from my past. Instead, I must change how I think about unchangeable past events.

6-5.   I must learn how to think about unchangeable past events only in God-I positive thoughts. Therein lies God's peace. When I learn how to do that, thoughts of my unchangeable past will never again destroy my present moment peace of mind.

CHAPTER SEVEN
Past Events Are Feelingless

7-1.   Past events have no feelings in and of themselves.

7-2.   What occurred in my past does not cause the feelings I have in the present moment.

7-3.   It is by dwelling upon Satan-I negative thoughts about a feelingless past event that causes me to feel upset, immobilized, or discontented in the present moment.

7-4.   By utilizing SOAP, I can wash away all Satan-I negative thoughts about a feelingless past event, which brings me to peace with that feelingless past event.

7-5.   I alone am responsible for letting thoughts of a nonexistent, immutable, feelingless past event destroy my present moment peace of mind. I alone am responsible if I am not free from my feelingless past!

CHAPTER EIGHT
Blame and Responsibility

8-1.   Societal blame is good. It is indispensable for maintaining an orderly society that guarantees its members life, liberty, and the pursuit of happiness.

8-2.   Subjective blame is vile. It is one of the greatest weapons Satan-I uses to destroy my enduring peace of mind.

If Satan-I can lead me into a subjective blame state of mind, he owns me.

8-3.   Nothing from my past is to blame for my feeling of being unhappy in the present moment. If I feel unhappy in the present moment, I alone am to blame for my feeling of unhappiness. My feeling of unhappiness is due to my erroneous Satan-I subjective blame stinking-thinking.

8-4.   At all costs, I must forever eradicate subjective blame from my thinking process. I will never again blame anyone or anything for how I feel in the present moment.

8-5.   By controlling my thought dwelling, I prevent Satan-I thoughts of subjective blame from ever causing me unhappiness in the present moment. That will bring me to enduring peace of mind. That will raise me to a higher level of consciousness.

CHAPTER NINE
What Another Person Did to You in Your Past Does Not Determine How You Feel in the Present Moment

9-1.   It is not at all important what another person did to me in my past. It is most important what thoughts I dwell upon relating to what that person did to me in my past.

9-2.   I alone am responsible for how I feel every conscious moment of my life, regardless of the injustices other people perpetrated upon me in my past.

9-3.   When I hate someone, I do not hurt the person I hate, I only hurt myself.

9-4.   When I feel angry about what that person did to me, I must admit that I am allowing Satan-I negative thoughts of my nonexistent, immutable, and feelingless past to interfere with my present moment peace of mind.

9-5.   In working my way through my healing, I use Stop, Obliterate, Alter, Praise when I experience Satan-I negative thoughts about the event or person. I deliberately *only* dwell upon God-I positive thoughts about the event or person. By doing that, I work through my hurt, I *deal* with the hurt. I get it *behind* me. I get on *with* my life. I *slay* the Other People Dragon! I am the victor!

Chapter Ten
Forgiving Yourself for Your Past Mistakes

10-1.   I am fallible. I made mistakes in the past. I will make mistakes in the future. Of that I am certain.

10-2.   What I did, I did. It's over. It's done. It is immutable. I cannot change any past mistakes one iota. However, I realize there is no connection between any of my past mistakes and how I feel in the present moment. I realize that although I can never change any past mistake, I can change the manner in which I think about any past mistake.

10-3.   What I did was stupid. However, I am not stupid. I am not any past mistake. I am not *it*. *It* is not me. I am not the same person who made that stupid mistake. I am a loved child of God. That is a distinction God never wants me to forget.

10-4.   I know the nanosecond I ask God to forgive me for any past stupid mistake, it is forgiven. God then wants me to forgive myself. It is my duty to obey God's command. It is my duty to forgive myself for all my past mistakes.

10-5.   I must think about all my past mistakes only in God-I positive thoughts. I must immediately SOAP away any Satan-I negative thought about a past mistake. That will allow me to slay the Me Dragon and bring me to peace with my past mistakes. I will never forget, "Historical or emotional?"

CHAPTER ELEVEN
What Fate Did to You in Your Past Does Not Determine How You Feel in the Present Moment

11-1. What Fate did to me does not determine how I feel in the present moment.

11-2. I alone am responsible for how I feel every conscious moment of my life, regardless of what Fate did to me.

11-3. If other people can recover from their Fate traumas, it irrefutably proves to me that I, too, can recover from the trauma of what Fate did to me, if I want to.

11-4. I use Stop, Obliterate, Alter, Praise when I am experiencing Satan-I negative thoughts about the hand Fate dealt me. I deliberately choose only to dwell upon God-I positive thoughts when I think about the hand that Fate dealt me. By doing that, I viciously slay the Fate Dragon.

11-5. Mighty men and women are mightily tormented and tenaciously arise unscathed with their enduring peace of mind intact.

About the Author

Michael Sage Hider obtained a BS degree in Metallurgical Engineering from the University of Cincinnati, an MA degree in Philosophy from the University of Toledo, and a Juris Doctor degree from the University of Santa Clara. He also pursued studies at Ohio State, San Jose State, and Stanford Universities.

As an Air Force Officer he conducted hypervelocity impact studies at Eglin Air Force Base and underground nuclear tests at the Nevada Test Site. He then became a silicon crystal growing engineer for Fairchild Semiconductor Co. At Lockhead Missiles and Space Co., he was an aerospace engineer, developing heat shield materials for Trident submarine missile re-entry bodies. He is co-author of a technical paper entitled *The Protection of Beryllium In A Salt-Moist Environment.*

Hider left engineering for a career in law. He was a trial attorney for eleven years, then ran for and was elected Superior Court Judge in Merced County, California. During terms as Presiding Judge, he oversees a master calender which includes civil, criminal, and juvenile cases.

Hider has taught courses in science, philosophy, and/or law at Merced Community College, Chapman College, and the University of San Francisco Master's Program.

He and his wife, Eileen, have as a family Jeff and Laurie and their children Alexandra and Zachary, Jennifer and John, Dr. Steven Sage and Nicole, and Melissa who is still awaiting her Knight in Shining Armor.

To order addtional copies of

Spiritual Healing

send $19.95 plus shipping and handling to

Books Etc.
P.O. Box 4888
Seattle, WA 98104

or have your credit card ready and call

(800) 917-BOOK

———⇒●《◉》●⇐———

To address any comments,
or to inquire about speaking engagements,
please write to:

Michael Sage Hider
P.O. Box 2446
Merced, CA 95344